Type 2 Diabetes Cookbook for Beginners

1300 Days of Quick and Mouth-Watering Recipes on a Budget for the Newly Diagnosed

Bonus: 28-Day Meal Plan

By

MATILDA GRIFFITH

© Copyright 2022 by Matilda Griffith - All rights reserved.

This book is intended to provide accurate and reliable information on the subject and issue discussed. The publication is offered with the idea that the publisher is not obligated to provide accounting, legally permissible, or qualified services. If legal or professional assistance is required, a practicing member of the profession should be contacted.

- From a Declaration of Principles approved and accepted by a Publishers and Associations Committee.

It is expressly prohibited to reproduce, duplicate, or transmit any portion of this publication, whether electronically or in printed form. No recording or storage of this publication is strictly permitted without the written approval of the publisher. We retain all rights.

The information supplied below is declared to be accurate and consistent, in that any liability incurred, whether due to inattention or otherwise, as a result of the use or abuse of any policies, processes, the recipient reader is entirely responsible for following the instructions provided inside. The publisher will not be held accountable under any circumstances for any harm, loss, or monetary loss caused directly or indirectly by the material included herein.

All copyrights not owned by the publisher belong to the authors.

The information included below is provided solely for informative reasons and is universal. The presentation of the information is without a contract or any type of guaranteed assurance.

The trademarks are utilized without the trademark owner's permission, and the trademarks are published without the trademark owner's permission or support. All brands and trademarks mentioned in this book are solely for clarification and are held by their respective owners, who are not linked with this publication.

TABLE OF CONTENTS

Introduction 10

Chapter 1: What is Diabetes? 11

    1.1 Types of diabetes 11

    1.2 How common is diabetes? 12

    1.3 What health problems can people with diabetes develop? 12

Chapter 2: Diabetic diet and 28-Days Diet plan 13

    2.1 Why do you need to develop a healthy eating plan? 13

    2.2 What does a diabetes diet involve? 14

    2.3 Foods to avoid 15

    2.4 Meal Plan Week-by-week for 28 days 16

Chapter 3: Snack, Drinks, and Appetizers Recipes 20

    3.1 Bread Upma 20

    3.2 Soya Kebabs 21

    3.3 Oat Biscuits 21

    3.4 Spiced Pecans 22

    3.5 Savory Date & Pistachio Bites 22

    3.6 Flourless Blender Zucchini Muffins 23

    3.7 Baked Broccoli-Cheddar Quinoa Bites 23

    3.8 Apricot-Ginger Energy Balls 24

    3.9 Quark & Cucumber Toast 24

    3.10 Baked Chili-Lime Zucchini Chips 25

    3.11 Super-Seed Snack Bars 25

    3.12 Cherry-Cocoa-Pistachio Energy Balls 26

    3.13 Air-Fryer Crispy Chickpeas 26

    3.14 Pizza Bites 27

    3.15 Chili-Lime Brussels Sprout Chips 27

    3.16 Cinnamon-Sugar Pumpkin Seeds 28

    3.17 Carrot Cake Energy Bites 28

    3.18 Sweet & Spicy Wasabi Snack Mix 29

    3.19 Peaches & Cream Mini Muffins 29

    3.20 Pumpkin Coconut Energy Balls 30

    3.21 Air-Fryer Sweet Potato Chips 31

    3.22 Strawberry Planks 31

3.23 Spiced Crackers	31
3.24 Pea Pods with Dipping Sauces	32
3.25 Fruit Energy Balls	32
3.26 Ranch Pumpkin Seeds	33
3.27 PB & J Poppers	33
3.28 Cheesy party bake	34
3.29 Stuffed mini peppers	34
3.30 Guacamole deviled eggs	35
3.31 Parmesan spinach dip	35
3.32 Cheesy stuffed mushrooms	36
3.33 Caesar salad cups	36
3.34 Mini crab cakes	37
3.35 Cheesy mushroom flatbread	37
3.36 Mozzarella-asparagus roll-ups	38
3.37 Smoked salmon rounds	38
3.38 Healthy 7-layer dip	39
3.39 Speedy salmon croquettes	39
3.40 Cranberry-nut spread	40
3.41 Veggie-stuffed mushrooms	40
3.42 Baked sesame shrimp	41
3.43 Cheesy artichoke dip	42
3.44 Taco shrimp bites	42
3.45 Sun-dried tomato pesto dip	43
3.46 Baked jalapeno poppers	43
3.47 Crunchy blue cheese stuffers	44
3.48 Hot Diggity dog "bites"	44
3.49 Crunchy chicken nibblers	45
3.50 Creamy fiesta bites	45
3.51 Teriyaki cocktail meatballs	46
3.52 Southern deviled eggs	46
3.53 Easy cucumber cups	47
3.54 Italian style caponata	47
3.55 Bistro stuffed tomato bites	48
3.56 Zesty sausage meatballs	48
3.57 Hot 'n' crispy zucchini bites	49
3.58 Chicken & Vegetable Penne with Parsley-Walnut Pesto	49
3.59 Spinach, Apple & Chicken Salad with Poppy Seed Dressing & Cheese Crisps	50

3.60 Hazelnut-Parsley Roast Tilapia 51

3.61 Charred Vegetable & Bean Tostadas with Lime Crema 51

3.62 Chicken Enchilada Skillet Casserole 52

3.63 Low-Carb Cauliflower Fried Rice with Shrimp 53

3.64 Lemon Chicken & Rice 54

3.65 Pumpkin Seed Salmon with Maple-Spice Carrots 54

3.66 Salmon Couscous Salad 55

3.67 Vegan Cauliflower Fettuccine Alfredo with Kale 56

3.68 Curried Sweet Potato & Peanut Soup 56

3.69 Spinach & Strawberry Salad with Poppy Seed Dressing 57

3.70 Chicken & Cucumber Lettuce Wraps with Peanut Sauce 57

3.71 Tofu & Snow Pea Stir-Fry with Peanut Sauce 58

3.72 Chicken & Sun-Dried Tomato Orzo 59

3.73 Easy Pea & Spinach Carbonara 59

3.74 Sweet Potato-Black Bean Burgers 60

3.75 Curried Chickpea Stew 61

3.76 Pork & Green Chile Stew 61

3.77 Trapanese Pesto Pasta & Zoodles with Salmon 62

3.78 Maple-Roasted Chicken Thighs with Sweet Potato Wedges and Brussels Sprouts 63

3.79 Jambalaya Stuffed Peppers 63

3.80 Ginger Beef Stir-Fry with Peppers 64

3.81 Pork Skewers with Fruit Glaze 65

3.82 Red Cabbage-Apple Cauliflower Gnocchi 66

3.83 Chicken-Spaghetti Squash Bake 66

3.84 Vegetarian Stuffed Cabbage 67

3.85 Pesto Shrimp Pasta 68

Chapter 4: Breakfast Recipes 70

4.1 Scallion Grits with Shrimp 70

4.2 Flourless Savory Cheddar Zucchini Muffins 71

4.3 Mini Corn, Cheese and Basil Frittatas 71

4.4 No-Bake Blueberry Almond Energy Snacks 72

4.5 Healthy Bagel Toppings, 4 ways 73

4.6 Mushroom Freezer Breakfast Burritos 74

4.7 Vegetarian Lentils with Toasted Egg Recipe 75

4.8 High Protein Oatmeal 76

4.9 Whole Wheat Blueberry Muffins 76

4.10 Mixed Berry Smoothie 77

4.11 Quinoa Breakfast Bowl 77

4.12 Whole Grain Banana Pancakes 78

4.13 Hawaiian Hash 79

4.14 Classic Avocado Toast 79

4.15 Buttermilk Pumpkin Waffles 80

4.16 Southwest Breakfast Wraps 80

4.17 Lance's French Toast 81

4.18 Whole Wheat Pecan Waffles 81

4.19 Portobello Mushrooms Florentine 82

4.20 Apple Walnut Pancakes 83

4.21 Mixed Fruit with Lemon-Basil Dressing 83

4.22 Flaxseed Oatmeal Pancakes 84

4.23 Confetti Scrambled Egg Pockets 84

4.24 Whole Wheat Pancakes 85

4.25 Chicken Brunch Bake 86

4.26 Shakshuka 86

4.27 Chilled Overnight Chia 87

4.28 Classic Omelet and Greens 88

4.29 Berry Yogurt Bowl 89

4.30 Best-Ever Granola 89

4.31 Sheet Pan Sausage and Egg Breakfast Bake 90

4.32 Tofu Scramble 91

4.33 Pumpkin Protein Pancakes 91

4.34 Avocado Toast Recipe (with Pickled Onions) (Vegan + Best Tips) 92

4.35 Sweet Potato Kale Frittata 93

4.36 Gruyere, Bacon, and Spinach Scrambled Eggs 93

4.37 Easy Sausage & Pepper Skillet (Paleo, Whole30, Gluten-Free) 94

4.38 Fruity Yogurt Parfait 94

Chapter 5 Lunch Recipes 96

5.1 Curried Chicken Skillet 96

5.2 Pressure-Cooker Pork Tacos with Mango Salsa 97

5.3 Chicken with Peach-Avocado Salsa 97

5.4 Pressure-Cooker Italian Shrimp 'n' Pasta 98

5.5 Tuna Teriyaki Kabobs 99

5.6 Chicken & Spanish Cauliflower "Rice" 100

5.7 Grilled Chicken Chopped Salad 100

5.8 Fish Tacos with Berry Salsa 101

5.9 Chicken with Fire-Roasted Tomatoes 101
5.10 Grilled Pork Noodle Salad 102
5.11 Naked Fish Tacos 103
5.12 Simple Sesame Chicken with Couscous 103
5.13 Mediterranean Grilled Chicken & Greens 104
5.14 Sesame Turkey Stir-Fry 104
5.15 Fish Tacos with Guacamole 105
5.16 Grilled Steak Salad with Tomatoes & Avocado 106
5.17 Summer Garden Fish Tacos 106
5.18 Tuna with Tuscan White Bean Salad 107
5.19 Chicken & Goat Cheese Skillet 108
5.20 Shrimp Orzo with Feta 108
5.21 Savory Braised Chicken with Vegetables 109
5.22 Garlic Tilapia with Spicy Kale 109
5.23 Chicken Tacos with Avocado Salsa 110
5.24 Healthy Tuscan Chicken 110
5.25 Spicy Turkey Tenderloin 111
5.26 Artichoke Ratatouille Chicken 111
5.27 Asian Lettuce Wraps 112
5.28 Grilled Jerk Shrimp Orzo Salad 113
5.29 Dee's Grilled Tuna with Greens 113
5.30 Lemon-Lime Salmon with Veggie Sauté 114
5.31 Refreshing Shrimp Salad 115
5.32 Savory Pork Salad 115
5.33 Cobb Salad Wraps 116
5.34 Pork Grapefruit Stir-Fry 116
5.35 Beef Brunch Bake 117
5.36 Cod with Hearty Tomato Sauce 117
5.37 Spicy Coconut Shrimp with Quinoa 118
5.38 Zippy Turkey Zoodles 119
5.39 Hearty Chicken Gyros 119
5.40 Tuscan Fish Packets 120
5.41 Slow-Cooked Italian Chicken 121
5.42 Chicken with Celery Root Puree 121
5.43 Tuscan Chicken and Beans 122
5.44 The Ultimate Fish Tacos 122
5.45 Indian Baked Chicken 123

Chapter 6: Dinner Recipes 124

- 6.1 Mediterranean low carb broccoli salad 124
- 6.2 Chicken veggies stir fry 125
- 6.3 Ground turkey sweet potato skillet 126
- 6.4 Vegetarian lentil tacos 126
- 6.5 Healthy general Tso's chicken 127
- 6.6 Banham chicken burger lettuce wraps 128
- 6.7 Lemon garlic salmon 129
- 6.8 Summery tomato & zucchini quinoa pizza 130
- 6.9 Mexican chopped salad 130
- 6.10 Mediterranean grilled salmon kabobs 132
- 6.11 Low carb zucchini lasagna 132
- 6.12 Easy quinoa salad 133
- 6.13 Cauliflower tacos 134
- 6.14 Slow cooker chicken noodle soup (a healthy meal option!) 135
- 6.15 No-cook zucchini noodles with pesto 136
- 6.16 Turkey-stuffed bell peppers 136
- 6.17 Tropical chicken cauliflower rice bowls 137
- 6.18 Slow-cooker pork chops 138
- 6.19 Sweet & tangy salmon with green beans 138
- 6.20 Spaghetti squash meatball casserole 139
- 6.21 Parmesan chicken with artichoke hearts 139
- 6.22 Salmon & spinach salad with avocado 140
- 6.23 Shrimp avocado salad 141
- 6.24 Pan-roasted chicken and vegetables 141
- 6.25 Spicy beef & pepper stir-fry 142
- 6.26 Pulled chicken sandwiches 143
- 6.27 Skillet pork chops with apples and onion 143
- 6.28 Ginger steak fried rice 144
- 6.29 Italian hot dish 145
- 6.30 Grilled beef chimichangas 145
- 6.31 In-a-pinch chicken and spinach 146
- 6.32 The Great Lasagna 146
- 6.33 Simple sesame chicken with couscous 147
- 6.34 Braised Pork Stew 148
- 6.35 Asparagus Nicoise Salad 148
- 6.36 Peppered tuna kabobs 149

6.37 Makeover Turkey Burgers with Peach Mayo 149
6.38 Sesame Turkey Stir-Fry... 150
6.39 Beef and Rice Stuffed Cabbage Rolls 151
6.40 Meaty Slow-Cooked Jambalaya 151
6.41 Slow Cooker Boeuf Bourguignon... 152
Conclusion 153

Introduction

A diabetic diet (also known as a diabetes meal) is a dietary guide for individuals who have diabetes that helps them plan when to eat snacks and meals and what kind of foods to ingest. The fact is, there's not one diabetic diet that is effective for all persons with the disease. Having good control of one's diabetes and keeping a healthy body weight and proper nutrition is the objective of any diabetic dietary pattern. This includes controlling one's blood cholesterol and glucose l levels and maintaining proper nutrition and healthy body weight.

Health care nutritionists and providers can guide you in developing the optimal meal plan to handle your diabetes at home. Nutritionists can assist you in locating recipes and culinary suggestions to assist you in meal preparation and planning and preparing meals.

There is no fixed diabetic meal suitable for all individuals with gestational, type 2, or 1 diabetes; therefore, there is no standard medication regimen appropriate for all individuals suffering from this disease. Various variables influence your diet habits, including gender and age, general exercise and activity level, any drugs you might be consuming (particularly insulin or any other prescription medications), & whether or not people are attempting to lose body weight, among others several other things.

With modest modifications to meal scheduling and quantity levels, most physicians and health care experts believe that individuals with diabetes may eat similar foods & meals like another member of their family. It is preferable to take in a range of foods in healthy eating, just as it is in any other healthy diet.

Chapter 1: What is Diabetes?

Diabetes is a disorder where the human body's blood glucose becomes too high, commonly known as blood sugar. Your primary energy source is blood glucose, which derives from the food that you consume. Insulin, a hormone secreted by your pancreas, helps absorb glucose in your cells for utilization as energy. Occasionally the body does not produce enough or any insulin, or it does not utilize it appropriately. Glucose persists in the body's circulation also does not reach the cells as a result.

Carrying excessive glucose in the blood may lead to issues with time. Although there's no treatment for diabetes, you can learn how to handle it and stay healthy.

Diabetes is often referred to as 'borderline diabetes' and 'a sugar touch.' Such phrases imply that one does not have diabetes and has a milder form of the disease, although diabetes affects everyone.

1.1 Types of diabetes

Type I, type II, and gestational diabetes are the three forms of diabetes.

Type 1 diabetes
The body cannot produce insulin if you have type 1 diabetes, and the immune system assaults and kills the pancreas' insulin-producing cells. Although Type 1 Diabetes is most frequently diagnosed in children, it may affect anybody. To remain alive, patients having type 1 diabetes must take insulin daily.

Type 2 diabetes

The body cannot produce or utilize insulin well in type 2 diabetes. Type II diabetes may appear at any age, including infancy. This form of diabetes, on the other hand, is more common in older individuals, and it is the most prevalent type.

Gestational diabetes
During pregnancy, certain females acquire gestational diabetes. This kind of diabetes usually disappears once the baby is delivered. Once you've experienced gestational diabetes, you're more likely to acquire type 2 diabetes later in life. Diabetes reported in the pregnancy may indeed be type 2.

Other types of diabetes
Monogenic diabetes—hereditary types of diabetes—and cystic fibrosis-related diabetes are two less frequent forms.

1.2 How common is diabetes?

Diabetes affected 30.6 million individuals in the US in 2015, accounting for 9.4% of the total population. Over one-fourth of them seem to be unaware that they have the illness. One in four individuals in the 65 has diabetes. In adult individuals, type II diabetes accounts for 90-95 % of occurrences.

Who has a higher risk of developing type 2 diabetes?
If you're 45 or older, have a family history with diabetes, or are overweight, the risk of developing type 2 diabetes is increased. Lack of regular physical exercise, race, and some health issues like hypertension may increase your risk of getting type 2 diabetes. If you have prediabetes or gestational diabetes while pregnant, you can acquire type 2 diabetes.

1.3 What health problems can people with diabetes develop?

High glucose levels in the blood might cause problems such as:
- kidney disease
- eye problems
- stroke
- nerve damage
- heart disease
- dental disease
- foot problems

You may take measures to reduce your risk of acquiring diabetic complications.

Chapter 2: Diabetic diet and 28-Days Diet plan

Eating healthy meals in moderation and keeping regular mealtimes are the hallmarks of a diabetic diet.

A diabetic diet is a low-fat, nutrient-dense eating regimen that's low in calories and fat. A healthy diet should include plenty of vegetables, fruits, and whole grains. A diabetic diet is the greatest way to eat for most people.

2.1 Why do you need to develop a healthy eating plan?

Patients with diabetes or prediabetes may be referred to a nutritionist to create a healthy meal plan. Your glucose is under control, you're in charge of your weight, and you're in control of risk factors for heart disease and increased blood pressure.

The more fat and calories you consume, the more likely your blood glucose levels may increase unfavorably. An increased level of blood glucose (hyperglycemia) that persists and can cause long-term issues such as heart, nerve and kidney damage if it is not controlled can occur if blood glucose levels are not under control.

Making intelligent food selections and recording your eating habits can help maintain your blood glucose levels within a safe range.

If you're trying to lose weight while managing diabetes, a diabetic diet may help you do it in a healthy and structured manner.

2.2 What does a diabetes diet involve?

A diabetic diet calls for three regular meals per day. This aids in the efficient use of insulin, whether produced naturally by the body or provided to you through prescription.

With the aid of a qualified dietician, you may design a diet that meets your specific health objectives, preferences, and lifestyle. And they may also give you advice on how to better your overall eating habits, picking appropriate food portions for your weight and the proper amount of exercise.

Carbs

Carbohydrates such as sugars and starches are digested and converted to blood glucose during the process of digestion. Make healthy carbs a priority, such as:

- Fruits
- Vegetables
- Whole grains

- Legumes, like peas and beans
- Low-fat dairy products, like cheese & milk

Fiber-rich foods

All portions of plants that the body cannot digest are included in dietary fiber. Dietary fiber helps manage levels of blood sugar by moderating how food is digested in the body. Fiber-rich foods include:

- Vegetables
- Fruits
- Nuts
- Legumes, like peas and beans
- Whole grains

Heart-healthy fish

Eat fish, especially fatty fish, at least two days a week to keep your heart healthy. Fish high in omega-3 such as mackerel, tuna, salmon, and sardines, may help avoid heart disease.

Polyunsaturated and monounsaturated fats are found in a variety of foods and may aid in lowering cholesterol. These include:

- Avocados
- Nuts
- Canola, peanut oils

2.3 Foods to avoid

A heart-healthy diet may be prevented by foods high in the following nutrients.

Saturated fats: Animal proteins like hot dogs, beef, bacon and sausage, should be avoided if possible. Limit the use of oils derived from coconut and palm kernels as well.

Trans fats: Trans fats may be present in processed foods, baked products, margarine sticks and shortening.

Cholesterol: Dietary sources of cholesterol include dairy products of high-fat and animal proteins, such as liver and egg yolks. Limit your cholesterol intake to 200 milligrams (mg) per day.

Sodium. Aim for a daily sodium intake of no more than 2,300 mg.

2.4 Meal Plan Week-by-week for 28 days

Days	Breakfast	Snack	Lunch	Snack	Dinner
1	Scallion grits with shrimp	Bread upma	Curried chicken skillet	Soya kebabs	Chicken veggies stir fry
2	Flourless savory cheddar zucchini muffins	Oat biscuits	Pressure-cooker pork tacos with mango salsa	Soya kebabs	Ground turkey sweet potato skillet
3	Mushroom freezer breakfast burritos	Baked chili-lime zucchini chips	Chicken & Spanish cauliflower "rice."	Red cabbage-apple cauliflower gnocchi	Fried chicken dinner & Angie's perfect dinner rolls
4	Vegetarian lentils with toasted egg	Cherry-cocoa-pistachio energy balls	Orange lunch & cheese quesadilla lunch	Smoked salmon rounds	Summery tomato & zucchini quinoa pizza
5	Quinoa breakfast bowl	Easy pea & spinach carbonara	Grilled steak salad with tomatoes & avocado	Air-fryer sweet potato chips	Slow cooker chicken noodle soup
6	Mixed fruit with lemon-basil dressing	Chicken-spaghetti squash bake	Shrimp orzo with feta	A cup of berries mixed & a cup of yogurt low-fat.	Turkey-stuffed bell peppers
7	Chilled overnight chia	Trapanese pesto pasta & zoodles with salmon	Artichoke ratatouille chicken	Carrot cake energy bites	Pan-roasted chicken and vegetables

Days	Breakfast	Snack	Lunch	Snack	Dinner
8	Pumpkin Protein Pancakes	A cup of berries mixed & a cup of yogurt low-fat.	Tuna with Tuscan White Bean Salad	Bistro stuffed tomato bites	Vegetarian lentil tacos
9	Fruity Yogurt Parfait	Air-Fryer Crispy Chickpeas	Asian Lettuce Wraps	Cherry-cocoa-pistachio energy balls	Slow-cooker pork chops
10	Southwest Breakfast Wraps	Bread upma	Garlic Tilapia with Spicy Kale	Cheesy party bake	Shrimp avocado salad
11	High Protein Oatmeal	Stuffed mini peppers	The Ultimate Fish Tacos	Air-Fryer Sweet Potato Chips	Grilled beef chimichangas
12	Buttermilk Pumpkin Waffles	Super-Seed Snack Bars	Tuscan Fish Packets	Chicken-spaghetti squash bake	In-a-pinch chicken & spinach
13	Confetti Scrambled Egg Pockets	Carrot cake energy bites	Hearty Chicken Gyros	Smoked salmon rounds	Power lasagna
14	Flaxseed Oatmeal Pancakes	Baked chili-lime zucchini chips	Refreshing Shrimp Salad	Soya kebabs	Makeover turkey burgers with peach mayo

Days	Breakfast	Snack	Lunch	Snack	Dinner
15	Spaghetti Squash Bake	Red cabbage-apple cauliflower gnocchi	Grilled Pork Noodle Salad	Taco shrimp bites	Lemon garlic salmon
16	Mini Corn, Cheese and Basil Frittatas	Cinnamon-Sugar Pumpkin Seeds	Chicken & Goat Cheese Skillet	Air-fryer sweet potato chips	Healthy general Tso's chicken
17	Shakshuka	Creamy fiesta bites	Dee's Grilled Tuna with Greens	Chili-Lime Brussels Sprout Chips	Parmesan chicken with artichoke hearts
18	Whole Wheat Pecan Waffles	Hot 'n' crispy zucchini bites	Tuscan Chicken and Beans	Easy pea & spinach carbonara	No-cook zucchini noodles with pesto
19	Portobello Mushrooms Florentine	Mini crab cakes	Spicy Coconut Shrimp with Quinoa	Guacamole deviled eggs	Spicy beef & pepper stir-fry
20	Lance's French Toast	Mozzarella-asparagus roll-ups	Cobb Salad Wraps	Strawberry Planks	Low carb zucchini lasagna
21	Berry Yogurt Bowl	Oat biscuits	Naked Fish Tacos	Sweet & Spicy Wasabi Snack Mix	Slow cooker boeuf bourguignon

Days	Breakfast	Snack	Lunch	Snack	Dinner
22	Whole Wheat Blueberry Muffins	Trapanese pesto pasta & zoodles with salmon	Fish Tacos with Guacamole	Chicken-spaghetti squash bake	Mediterranean low carb broccoli salad
23	Whole Grain Banana Pancakes	Pizza Bites	Fish Tacos with Berry Salsa	Smoked salmon rounds	Tropical chicken cauliflower rice bowls
24	Sweet Potato Kale Frittata	Quark & Cucumber Toast	Healthy Tuscan Chicken	Cinnamon-Sugar Pumpkin Seeds	Cauliflower tacos
25	Mixed Berry Smoothie	Carrot Cake Energy Bites	Savoury Braised Chicken with Vegetables	Easy pea & spinach carbonara	Sesame turkey stir-fry
26	Healthy Bagel Toppings, 4 ways	Cheesy mushroom flatbread	Chicken with Celery Root Puree	Soya kebabs	Meaty slow-cooked jambalaya
27	Avocado Toast Recipe	Spiced Crackers	Zippy Turkey Zoodles	Cheesy mushroom flatbread	Pulled chicken sandwiches
28	Classic Avocado Toast	Trapanese pesto pasta & zoodles with salmon	Slow-Cooked Italian Chicken	Chili-Lime Brussels Sprout Chips	Easy quinoa salad

Chapter 3: Snack, Drinks, and Appetizers Recipes

3.1 Bread Upma

Prepping time: 8 minutes, Cooking Time: 20 mins, Servings: 2

Ingredients

- 8 to 11 slices of whole wheat bread
- 1 onion
- ½ cup tomato
- ½ tsp. green chili paste
- ½ tsp. ginger paste
- ½ tsp. turmeric
- ½ tsp. salt
- 8 curry leaves
- 1 tbsp. coriander leaves
- ½ tsp. mustard seeds
- ½ tsp. cumin seeds
- Oil and butter for frying purposes

Directions

1. In the pan, heat 1 tsp of oil. Mix the cumin and mustard. Continue to stir until the mustard seeds begin to sputter and the cumin color becomes reddish.
2. Add the turmeric to the roasted seeds.
3. Fry chopped onion and curry leaves in a pan with butter. Toss in the green chili paste, as well as tomato.
4. Keep stirring for 5 mins.
5. Toss inside bread cubes gently, but not that much, or it may get mushy. Cook for another 5 mins before adding green coriander.
6. Check that the bread cubes and paste are well mixed.
7. Serve hot immediately.

Nutritional Facts:
Calories: 336 Kcal Proteins: 7.3 g Fats: 6 g Carbs: 42.6 g

3.2 Soya Kebabs

Prepping time: 15mins, Cooking Time: 15 mins, Servings: 4

Ingredients

- 2 cups soya chunks, soaked and drained
- 1 large onion, chopped
- 2 green chilies, cut
- 1 cup coriander leaves
- 150g tofu, grated
- 3 tbsp. sago
- ½ cup flat rice (pressed rice), boiled
- 1 tsp. coriander powder
- 1 tsp. cumin powder
- ½ tsp. red chili powder
- ¼ tsp. dry mango powder
- Ginger (grated) to taste
- Salt to taste
- Oil for frying

Directions

1. Mix onion, soya, chilies, coriander powder, chili powder, mango powder, ginger, and salt in a blender for 15 seconds.
2. Add tofu and blend for another 2 mins.
3. Remove from the blender and place in a bowl with pressed rice, sago, and coriander leaves. Mix well.
4. Form the mixture into small balls, as big or small as you want the kebabs to be.
5. Heat the oil and add approximately at a time three balls of the mixture in a pan. Fry the ball mixture until golden brown on both sides, then transfer on tissue paper.
6. Serve hot with chutney or sauce.

Nutritional Facts
Calories: 345 Kcal Proteins: 52 g Fats: 0.5 g Carbs: 33 g

3.3 Oat Biscuits

Cooking Time: 25 mins, Prepping time: 20 mins, Servings: 5

Ingredients

- 1 ½ cups whole wheat flour
- 6 tbsp. rolled oats
- ½ cup all-purpose flour
- ½ cup sweetener
- 1 tsp. baking powder
- 1 tsp. salt
- 4 tbsp. low fat butter
- ½ cup skimmed milk

Directions

1. Heat the oven to 350°Farhienhiet and butter a baking pan.
2. Make a fine powder out of the rolled oats by pulsing in a food processor.
3. Put the all-purpose flour, whole wheat flour, baking powder, and salt in a mixing bowl and whisk until smooth. This is where you'll add oats, sweetener, and salt.

4. While using an electric mixer, gradually incorporate the butter into the batter. To make the mixture adhere together, add milk a third at a time.
5. Make rounds out of the dough, approximately 3" thick.
6. To prevent the cookies from bursting in the oven, place them on baking pans and poke holes within the dough to prevent them from sticking together.
7. Bake for approximately 15 mins or until golden brown.

Nutritional Facts:
Calories: 81 Kcal Proteins: 1.12 g Fats: 3.26 g Carbs: 12.37 g

3.4 Spiced Pecans

Cooking Time: 70 mins, Prepping time: 20 mins, Servings: 4
Ingredients
- 1 egg white
- 1 tbsp. water
- 6 tbsp. superfine sugar
- ½ tsp. kosher salt
- ¼ tsp. ground allspice
- ¼ tsp. ground cloves
- ¼ tsp. ground nutmeg
- Pinch of ground cinnamon
- Pinch of cayenne pepper
- 4 cups pecan halves

Directions
1. Preheat the oven to 275 degrees Fahrenheit. Wrap parchment paper around a rimmed baking sheet.
2. In a large mixing pot, whisk together egg whites, sugar, water, salt, cloves, allspice, nutmeg, cayenne pepper, and cinnamon. Mix pecans and stir until fully incorporated. Pour the batter into the pan in a single layer.
3. After baking for 30 mins, change the pan's position from front to back and keep baking until the nuts become crispy and dry to the touch. Cool for 30 mins, then break apart and serve for eating.

Nutritional Facts:
Calories: 114.4 Kcal Proteins: 1.5 g Fats: 9.7 g Carbs: 7.2 g

3.5 Savory Date & Pistachio Bites

Prepping time: 10 mins, Cooking Time: 15mins, Servings: 2
Ingredients
- 2 cups pitted whole dates
- Cup of raw pistachios, unsalted and shelled
- Cup of golden raisins
- 1 tsp. ground fennel seeds
- 1/4 tsp. powdered pepper

Directions
1. In the food processor, add the dates, pepper, raisins, pistachios, and fennel.
2. Make 32 balls from this mixture after chopping all ingredients in the processor.

Nutritional Facts
Calories: 68 Kcal Proteins: 1.1 g Fats: 1.8 g Carbs: 13.4 g

3.6 Flourless Blender Zucchini Muffins

Cooking Time: 20 mins, Prepping time: 10 mins, Servings: 3

Ingredients

- 1 ½ cups rolled oats
- 1 tsp. baking powder
- ½ tsp. ground cinnamon
- ¼ tsp. baking soda
- ¼ tsp. salt
- 1 medium zucchini
- 2 large eggs
- ⅓ cup brown sugar
- 3 tbsp. canola oil
- 1 tsp. vanilla extract
- ½ cup mini-choco chips (optional)

Directions

1. Preheat the oven to 350°F. Using a cooking spray, coat a 24-cup mini muffin pan.
2. Blend the oats until they are gently ground. Blend 1-2 times. Combine cinnamon powder, baking powder, baking soda, and salt. Sautee until smooth.
3. Toss in mini-choco chips. Fill muffin cases halfway with batter.
4. Bake the batter for 15-17 mins or until a toothpick comes out clean. Cool for five mins on the wire rack.

Nutritional Facts:
Calories: 108 Kcal Proteins: 2.5 g Fats: 1.2 g Carbs: 13.5 g

3.7 Baked Broccoli-Cheddar Quinoa Bites

Cooking Time: 40 mins, Prepping time: 15 mins, Servings: 5

Ingredients

- ½ cup of quinoa
- ⅛ tsp. salt + ¼ tsp. salt (separated)
- ¾ cup finely chopped broccoli
- ¾ cup grated cheddar cheese
- ½ tsp. baking powder
- ½ tsp. garlic powder
- ¼ tsp. onion powder
- ¼ tsp. ground pepper
- 1 large beaten egg
- Cooking oil spray

Directions

1. Preheat oven to 350°F. Coat the 16 cups of the muffin pan using cooking spray.
2. Follow the package directions to cook the quinoa with the ⅛ tsp salt. Take off the heat, cover it and then let it cool for 5 mins.
3. Allow it cool at least for 10 mins inside the large mixing basin.

4. Toss in quinoa with the cheddar cheese, broccoli, baking powder, pepper, onion powder, garlic powder, and other 1/4 teaspoon salt. Add the egg and mix well.
5. Using slightly wet fingertips, push all quinoa mixture gently into the lined muffin pans. Sprinkle the top with cooking oil spray
6. Bake for 22-25 mins, or till the color is golden brown. Set aside to cool for about 20 mins in the dish on a cooling rack, then transfer to the pan to cool entirely.

Nutritional Facts
Calories: 87 Kcal Proteins: 4.6 g Fats: 4.2 g Carbs: 7.8 g

3.8 Apricot-Ginger Energy Balls

Cooking Time: 30 mins, Prepping time: 10 mins, Servings: 7
Ingredients
- 1 ½ cups dried apricots
- ¾ cup rolled oats
- ¾ cup fine grated unsweetened coconut
- 6 tbsp. tahini
- 3 tbsp. honey
- ¾ tsp. ground ginger
- Pinch of a salt

Directions
1. Mix the oats, apricots, coconut, salt, honey, and ginger in the food processor.
2. Blend 10-20 times until ingredients are finely chopped, then continue for one minute, wiping down both sides as required until the texture looks flaky and can be shaped into a compact mass.
3. Squeeze approximately 1 tbsp of the mixture gently into your palms and shape it into a ball using moist fingers (to avoid the mixture from adhering to fingers).
4. Put in a vessel for preservation. Repeat the procedure with the remaining mixture.

Nutritional Facts:
Calories: 57 Kcal Proteins: 1.1 g Fats: 2.9 g Carbs: 7.8 g

3.9 Quark & Cucumber Toast

Cooking Time: 10 mins, Prepping time: 5 mins, Servings: 2
Ingredients
- 1 slice toasted whole-grain bread
- 2 tbsp. quark
- 2 tbsp. diced cucumber
- 1 tbsp. cilantro leaves
- Pinch of sea salt

Directions
1. Coat the toasted bread with cucumber, cilantro leaves, quark, cilantro, and sea salt.

Nutritional Facts:

Calories: 141 Kcal Proteins: 7.6 g Fats: 5.1 g Carbs: 13.8 g

3.10 Baked Chili-Lime Zucchini Chips

Prepping time: 20 mins, Cooking Time: 120 mins, Servings: 5

Ingredients

- 2 medium-sized zucchinis, cut into pieces
- Cooking oil spray
- 2 tsp. lime juice
- ¼ tsp. chili powder
- ¼ tsp. salt

Directions

1. Heat the oven to approximately 225°F, with racks in the top and the bottom thirds. Use the parchment paper to line 2 large baking sheets.
2. Cut 0.12-inch-thick pieces of zucchini. Place one layer of the slices on the prepared parchment paper and wipe using a towel.
3. Coat generously using cooking spray. Do not make pieces overlap each other.
4. Add a bit of salt and chilli powder and lime juice to the dish.
5. Bake for 60 mins, rotating pans midway through. Bake it for another 45-55 minutes, or until the zucchini pieces are golden and not wet.
6. Monitor after that period and eliminate any dark pieces which are cooked. Place cooked zucchini crisps on a cooling rack to cool.

Nutritional Facts:
Calories: 72 Kcal Proteins: 2.5 g Fats: 4.3 g Carbs: 7.7 g

3.11 Super-Seed Snack Bars

Prepping time: 20 mins, Cooking Time: 40 mins, Servings: 3

Ingredients

- ⅓ cup tahini
- ⅓ cup honey
- 1 tsp. vanilla extract
- ¼ tsp. salt
- 1 cup grated unsweetened coconut
- ½ cup raw saltless pepitas
- ½ cup saltless sunflower seeds
- ¼ cup chia seeds
- ¼ cup hemp seeds

Directions

1. Heat the oven to approximately 225 °F, with racks in the top and the bottom thirds. Use the parchment paper to line 2 large baking sheets.
2. Mix honey and tahini in a saucepan over medium heat.
3. Keep stirring for approximately two mins, or until well blended and heated. Whisk in the salt and vanilla after having removed the pan from the heat.

4. Add pepitas, coconut, sunflower seeds, hemp seeds and chia seeds to the mixing pan.
5. Toss in tahini until everything is uniformly covered.
6. Press down all ingredients firmly.
7. Bake for 30-35 mins, or until brown. Allow cooling on a cooling rack.
8. Take the leftover squares out with overhanging parchment. Slice into 25 cubes using a utensil.

Nutritional Facts:
Calories: 110 Kcal Proteins: 3.4 g Fats: 8.5 g Carbs: 7 g

3.12 Cherry-Cocoa-Pistachio Energy Balls

Cooking Time: 30 mins, Prepartion time: 10 mins, Servings: 3

Ingredients
- 1 ½ cups dried cherries
- ¾ cup shelled salted pistachios
- ½ cup almond butter
- 3 tbsp. cocoa powder
- 4 tbsp. maple syrup
- ½ tsp. ground cinnamon

Directions
1. Blend all pistachios, almond butter, cherries, cocoa powder, cinnamon, and maple syrup in a hand blender. Blend 10-20 times till mixture becomes finely chopped, then continue for another 1 min, wiping down sides as needed, until powdery but can still be formed into a firm ball.
2. Compress approximately 1 tbsp of the mixture between both palms firmly and shape into a ball using moist hands (to avoid the mixture from adhering to them). Place the jar in a safe place. Using the leftover mixture, repeat the process.

Nutritional Facts
Calories: 72 Kcal Proteins: 1.6 g Fats: 3.7 g Carbs: 9.2 g

3.13 Air-Fryer Crispy Chickpeas

Cooking Time: 15 mins, Prepping time: 10 mins, Servings: 2

Ingredients
- 1 (15 ounces) can chickpeas, washed and drained
- 1 ½ tbsp. toasted sesame oil
- ¼ tsp. smoked paprika
- ¼ tsp. crushed red pepper
- ⅛ tsp. salt
- Cooking spray
- 2 slices of lime

Directions

1. Put chickpeas on paper towels and cover them with a dish towel to prevent them from drying out. Pat the chickpeas dry with paper towels, rolling them beneath the towels to ensure they are dry on all sides.
2. Put chickpeas in a bowl and combine with oil. Add paprika, powdered red pepper, and kosher salt to taste. Coat the basket of the air fryer using cooking spray before adding the mixture. Cook, stirring the basket periodically, at 400°F until nicely browned, 12-14 mins. Serve the chickpeas with lime wedges squeezed over them.

Nutritional Facts:
Calories: 132 Kcal Proteins: 4.7 g Fats: 5.8 g Carbs: 14.1 g

3.14 Pizza Bites

Cooking Time: 15 mins, Prep time: 10 mins, Servings: 2

Ingredients
- 4 split multi-grain sandwich thins
- ½ cup tomato sauce
- 1 tsp. Italian seasoning
- ¼ tsp. crushed red pepper
- 3 ounces thinly sliced smoked turkey sausage
- ½ cup yellow pepper, chopped
- 3 ounces shredded mozzarella cheese, part-skim

Directions
1. Set the oven to 400°F. Bake the sandwich-thin on a parchment-lined baking sheet. Five mins in the oven should be enough.
2. Combine tomato sauce with Italian seasoning and red pepper inside a separate small bowl. Spread the sauce mix over the sandwich thins. Add a layer of sausage and bell pepper on top for some more flavor. Add a little cheese to finish it off. Bake for 8 mins until the cheese is melted and bubbling. Add more Italian seasoning, if desired.

Nutritional Facts:
Calories: 44 Kcal Proteins: 1.2 g Fats: 1.3 g Carbs: 6.8 g

3.15 Chili-Lime Brussels Sprout Chips

Prepping time: 15 mins, Cooking Time: 15 mins, Servings: 2

Ingredients
- 1 lb. brussels sprouts
- 1 tbsp. olive oil
- ½ tsp. chili powder
- ½ tsp. shredded lime zest
- ¼ tsp. ground pepper
- ⅛ tsp. salt
- 1 tsp. lime juice
- Butter for cooking

Directions
1. Set the oven to 300°F.

2. On a baking sheet, scatter the pumpkin seeds evenly. Allow baking for 40 mins, stirring once.
3. In a medium bowl, add sugar, salt, and cinnamon. Turn off the oven and transfer pumpkin seeds to a bowl. Stir seeds in the beaten egg white and butter. Coat the pumpkin seeds in the sugar mixture. Transfer the baking sheet back in the oven and distribute an equal layer of the batter over the top of it. Bake for 10 to 20 mins, or until the top is just beginning to turn golden. Before serving, allow to cool fully.

Nutritional Facts:
Calories: 45 Kcal Proteins: 0.9 g Fats: 3.6 g Carbs: 2.6 g

3.16 Cinnamon-Sugar Pumpkin Seeds

Prepping time: 15 mins, Cooking Time: 15 mins, Servings: 2

Ingredients
- 2 cups pumpkin seeds
- 1 tbsp. sugar
- ½ tsp. ground cinnamon
- ¼ tsp. salt
- 1 egg
- 2 tbsp. melted butter

Directions
1. In a food processor, mix pecans, dates, oats, & chia seeds till they are thoroughly mixed and diced.
2. Process the carrots, salt, vanilla, ginger, cinnamon, turmeric, and pepper until the mixture becomes a smooth paste.
3. Roll 1 tbs of the mixture into balls.

Nutritional Facts:
Calories: 107 Kcal Proteins: 5.1 g Fats: 9.4 g Carbs: 2.6 g

3.17 Carrot Cake Energy Bites

Prepping time: 15 mins, Cooking Time: 20 mins, Servings: 2

Ingredients
- 1 cup dates
- ½ cup rolled oats
- ¼ cup of chopped pecans
- ¼ cup chia seeds
- 2 medium carrots
- 1 tsp. vanilla extract
- ¾ tsp. ground cinnamon
- ½ tsp. ground ginger
- ¼ tsp. ground turmeric
- ¼ tsp. salt
- Pinch of freshly ground pepper

Directions:
1. Make a smooth puree out of the ingredients by blending them in a food processor; season to taste with nutmeg or cayenne pepper before serving.

2. Make little balls out of the mixture, each comprising of just 1 tbsp.

Nutritional Facts:
Calories: 96 Kcal Proteins: 1.8 g Fats: 3.4 g Carbs: 16.6 g

3.18 Sweet & Spicy Wasabi Snack Mix

Prepping time: 10 mins, Cooking Time: 15 mins, Servings: 2

Ingredients
- 2 ½ cups crispy corn & rice cereal
- 2 cups pretzel sticks
- 1 cup dried peas
- ¾ cup almonds
- ¼ cup butter
- 2 tbsp. rice vinegar
- 4 tsp. sesame seeds
- 1 tbsp. soy sauce
- ½ tsp. ground ginger
- ¼ tsp. cayenne pepper
- ½ cup dried apricots

Directions
1. Set the oven to 300°F. Be sure to include the pretzel sticks, peas, cereal and almonds in a big mixing basin. Place the mixture aside.
2. Heat and whisk the butter until it melts in a saucepan with vinegar, toasted sesame seeds, ginger, cayenne pepper and soy sauce over medium-low heat. Gently combine the cereal and butter in a large bowl. Transfer everything to a 15x10 inch baking pan.
3. Bake for another 30 mins or more unless the mixture is nearly completely dried out, stirring twice during that time. Add the apricots and mix well. To cool, spread the batter out over a wide sheet of aluminum foil. Keep in a sealed jar for up to 3 days at room temperature or 1 month in the freezer.

Nutritional Facts:
Calories: 126 Kcal Proteins: 3.3 g Fats: 6.6 g Carbs: 15.2 g

3.19 Peaches & Cream Mini Muffins

Prepping time: 15 mins, Cooking Time: 20 mins, Servings: 2

Ingredients
- 2 ¼ cups flour
- 1 ½ tsp. baking powder
- ¼ tsp. salt
- 3 oz. cream cheese
- 1 cup sugar
- ⅔ cup milk
- 3 tbsp. yogurt
- 3 tbsp. canola oil
- 1 egg
- 1 ½ cups peach slices
- ¼ tsp. ground cinnamon
- 2 tbsp. butter

Directions

1. Set the oven to 375°F. Muffin cups may be used to line 53 3/4-inch muffin tins. Prepare the muffin cups by spraying with cooking spray and putting them aside. Prepping time is only a few mins because the batter is already mixed.
2. In a large dish, mix 3/4 cup of sugar, cream cheese, milk, yogurt, and oil. Use a mixer to combine the ingredients thoroughly. Add the egg and mix until everything is well combined. Pour flour into the mixture and whisk until it's moistened, perhaps 30 seconds or so. Add the peaches and combine well.
3. Stuff prepared muffin cups two-thirds of the way with butter.
4. In a separate dish, mix the remaining ¼ cup of flour, 1/4 cup of sugar, and the cinnamon. Spread butter in cups after cutting in butter with a pastry blender until the consistency is coarse crumbs.
5. Bake for 8 to 12 mins, or until the top begins to turn golden brown around the edges. Allow the muffins to cool for five mins in the cups on a cooling rack. Remove the muffins from the tins.

Nutritional Facts:
Calories: 56 Kcal Proteins: 1 g Fats: 2 g Carbs: 9 g

3.20 Pumpkin Coconut Energy Balls

Prepping time: 15 mins, Cooking Time: 25 mins, Servings: 2

Ingredients

- 1 ½ cups oats
- ½ cup slivered almonds
- ⅓ cup coconut
- ¾ cup canned pumpkin
- 2 tbsp. honey
- 2 tsp. pumpkin pie spice
- ¼ tsp. salt
- ⅛ tsp. cayenne pepper

Directions

1. Set the oven to 300°F.
2. Spread out the oats, coconut, and almonds on a baking sheet. Bake for 8-10 mins, turning one or two times. On the rack, let the ice cream cool to room temperature.
3. Add toasted oat mixture to a bowl and combine well.
4. Make 20 equal-sized balls out of the batter, each approximately 2 tsp in size. Assemble the balls and place them on a serving platter. It is best served right away, but it may be stored in the refrigerator for two days.

Nutritional Facts:
Calories: 114 Kcal Proteins: 3.1 g Fats: 5.4 g Carbs: 15.2 g

3.21 Air-Fryer Sweet Potato Chips

Prepping time: 10 mins, Cooking Time: 15 mins, Servings: 2

Ingredients

- 1 sweet potato, sliced
- 1 tbsp. canola oil
- ¼ tsp. salt
- ¼ tsp. ground pepper

Directions

1. Soak potato pieces for about 20 mins in cold water. To soak up the water, use paper towels and then pat dry.
2. Put the sweet potatoes in a dry dish. Sprinkle with salt and pepper and toss in the oil for coating.
3. To coat the air fryer basket, use cooking spray. Place a layer of sweet potatoes in a container. Flip and rearrange into layers for 5 mins while cooking at 350°F, unless cooked crispy (approximately 15 mins). With tongs, take the chips out of the air fryer and place them on a platter. Make sure to use up all the sweet potatoes before you go on to the next step.
4. To serve, allow chips to be cool for five mins before scooping out. You may also let them cool fully before storing them in a sealed jar for up to three days.

Nutritional Facts:
Calories: 84 Proteins: 1.2 g Fats: 3.6 g Carbs: 12.1 g

3.22 Strawberry Planks

Prepping time: 10 mins, Cooking Time: 15 mins, Servings: 2

Ingredients

- 2 graham cracker squares
- 2 tsp. cream cheese
- 2 strawberries, sliced
- 2 oz. crushed sugar

Directions

1. Make 4 rectangles from cracker squares by breaking them. Cheese should be distributed on rectangles in an equal layer. Place strawberry slices in the middle of every rectangle and position them as desired. Add a thin dusting of powdered sugar, if necessary.

Nutritional Facts:
Calories: 200 Kcal Proteins: 3 g Fats: 5 g Carbs: 34 g

3.23 Spiced Crackers

Prepping time: 10 mins, Cooking Time: 15 mins, Servings: 2

Ingredients

- 3 tbsp. olive oil
- 1 ½ tsp. ground paprika
- 1 ½ tsp. dried oregano
- Pinch of salt
- 3 cups pita chips

Directions
1. Set the oven to 300°F.
2. In a bowl, mix oil, salt, oregano, and paprika. Toss in crackers (or chips) once they've been added to the mixture. Put on a baking sheet with a raised rim. Ten mins in the oven should be enough. Allow cooling for 10 mins before removing from pan.

Nutritional Facts:
Calories: 20 Kcal Proteins: 1 g Fats: 0.1 g Carbs: 4 g

3.24 Pea Pods with Dipping Sauces

Prepping time: 12 mins, Cooking Time: 15 mins, Servings: 2

Ingredients
- 3 cups of pea pods
- 1 recipe of Sauce

Directions
1. In a saucepan, boil pea pods in boiling salted water for 2-4 mins.
2. Drain and let to cool. If necessary, chill. Serve with the honey mustard creamy sauce.

Nutritional Facts:
Calories: 80 Kcal Proteins: 10 g Fats: 4 g Carbs: 8 g

3.25 Fruit Energy Balls

Prepping time: 15 mins, Cooking Time: 20 mins, Servings: 2

Ingredients
- 1 cup almonds
- 1 cup figs
- 1 cup apricots
- ⅓ cup coconut

Directions
1. Mix the almonds, apricots, and figs in a food processor until they are chopped. Make tiny balls out of the mixture and roll in coconut before serving.

Nutritional Facts:
Calories: 70 Kcal Proteins: 1.5 g Fats: 3.3 g Carbs: 10.1 g

3.26 Ranch Pumpkin Seeds

Prepping time: 10 mins, Cooking Time: 15 mins, Servings: 2

Ingredients
- 2 cups pumpkin seeds
- 2 tbsp. buttermilk powder
- 1 tbsp. dried chives
- 2 tsp. dried dill
- 1 tsp. garlic powder
- 1 tsp. onion powder
- ½ tsp. salt
- ¼ tsp. ground pepper
- 1 egg

Directions
1. Set the oven to 300°F.
2. On a wide baking sheet, scatter the pumpkin seeds out evenly. Bake for about 40 mins, stirring occasionally.
3. In a bowl, mix buttermilk powder, dill, chives, and the rest of the seasonings. Put the pumpkin seeds carefully into a medium-sized basin. Mix the seeds in the egg to ensure they are well-coated. Mix in the buttermilk powder mixture until it is evenly distributed throughout. Distribute the seeds out evenly on the baking sheet once again. Continue baking for a further 15 min.

Nutritional Facts:
Calories: 95 Kcal Proteins: 5.4 g Fats: 8 g Carbs: 2.4 g

3.27 PB & J Poppers

Prepping time: 5 mins, Cooking Time: 10 mins, Servings: 2

Ingredients
- ⅓ cup cheese spread
- 1 tbsp. peanut butter
- ¼ tsp. ground ginger
- 12 small caramel rice cakes
- ¼ cup flavor you desire sugar-free preserves
- 2 tbsp. chocolate pieces

Directions
1. In a bowl, mix cream cheese, ginger, and peanut butter. Uniformly distributed over rice cakes. Add the preserves in an equal layer on top. Sprinkle additional chocolate shavings, if necessary.

Nutritional Facts:
Calories: 135 Kcal Proteins: 25 g Fats: 8 g Carbs: 16 g

3.28 Cheesy party bake

Prepping time: 10 mins, Cooking time: 10 mins, servings: 16

Ingredients

- 1/2 cup mayonnaise
- 2 cups Swiss cheese, shredded
- 1 tsp. garlic powder
- 1 scallion, thinly sliced
- Paprika for seasoning

Directions

1. Set the oven to 360°Fahrienhiet.
2. Except for paprika in a bowl, combine all ingredients.
3. Bake for 20-25 mins, or until brown and the cheese melts, in a 1-quart baking pan, sprinkled with paprika.

Nutritional Facts:
Calories: 143 Kcal Proteins: 34 g Fats: 6 g Carbs: 37 g

3.29 Stuffed mini peppers

Prepping time: 10 mins, Cooking time: 30 mins, servings: 10

Ingredients

- 1/2 lb. ground beef
- 1/2 cup white rice, cooked
- 1/2 cup salsa
- 1 tsp. onion powder
- 1 tsp. garlic powder
- 1/4 tsp. black pepper
- 1/2 lb. sweet peppers
- 1/4 cup cheddar cheese, shredded

Directions

1. Set the oven to 350°F. Apply cooking spray on the baking sheet.
2. Be sure to put all the ingredients in a bowl before mixing.
3. Spoon the mixture into the tiny peppers and distribute it evenly. Put it on a baking sheet and wrap it with aluminum foil to keep warm.
4. Bake for 25-30 mins, or until the meat is no longer pink. Put the cheese and bake for an additional 3 mins, or till the cheese melts.

Nutritional Facts:
Calories: 287 Kcal Proteins: 32 g Fats: 12 g Carbs: 28 g

3.30 Guacamole deviled eggs

Prepping time: 5 mins, Cooking time: 15 mins, servings: 12

Ingredients

- 6 boiled eggs
- 1 avocado
- 2 tbsp. red onion
- 1 tbsp. chopped cilantro
- 3 tbsp. mayonnaise
- 1 tbsp. lime juice
- 1/8 tsp. salt
- 1/8 tsp. black pepper

Directions

1. Mash egg yolks and avocado together in a mixing bowl. Make a dressing by combining the remaining ingredients in a bowl.
2. Place halved eggs on a dish and fill with yolk mixture. Refrigerate till ready to eat, then top with paprika and cover.

Nutritional Facts:
Calories: 323 Kcal Proteins: 29 g Fats: 13 g Carbs: 35 g

3.31 Parmesan spinach dip

Prepping time: 15 mins, Cooking time: 30 mins, servings: 14

Ingredients

- 2 packages frozen spinach, chopped
- 1 package softened cream cheese
- 1/2 cup parmesan cheese (reserve 1 tbsp for topping)
- 1/3 cup mayonnaise
- 2 tbsp. lemon juice
- 1 tsp. garlic powder
- 1 can of water chestnuts, sliced and chopped

Directions

1. Set the oven to 350°f. Using cooking spray, prepare a 2-quart casserole dish.
2. Beat spinach and cream cheese in a large bowl, reserving 1 tbsp. Add the parmesan cheese, mayonnaise, garlic powder and lemon juice until fully combined. Add water chestnuts and a spoon into a casserole dish that has been prepared. Add 1 tbsp of the reserved parmesan cheese on top and wrap it in aluminum foil to melt the cheese.
3. Bake the mixture for 15 mins in the oven, remove the foil and continue baking for 15 to 20 mins more, or until the food is cooked through. Prepare the food and serve it right away.

Nutritional Facts
Calories: 189 Kcal Proteins: 19 g Fats: 11 g Carbs: 20 g

3.32 Cheesy stuffed mushrooms

Prepping time: 10 mins, Cooking time: 25 mins, servings: 4

Ingredients

- 12 big mushrooms
- 2 tbsp. bell pepper, chopped
- 1 tbsp. chopped scallions
- 1 tbsp. cream cheese
- 1 tbsp. chopped parsley
- 2 tbsp. plain or seasoned bread crumbs
- 1/2 tsp. garlic powder
- 1/8 tsp. black pepper

Directions

1. Set the oven to 350°f. Spray cooking spray on baking sheet
2. Remove stems from the mushrooms and coarsely slice them. Place the mushroom caps on the baking sheet that has been prepared.
3. Cook the crushed red bell pepper, mushroom stems, and scallions for 2-3 mins on medium heat. Cook for 1-2 mins, stirring periodically, after adding the cream cheese, breadcrumbs, parsley, garlic powder, and black pepper.
4. The mixture should be poured equally into the mushroom caps and sprayed using cooking spray on the tops.
5. Cover and bake for around 15 mins. Bake for another 5-6 mins, or till the tops are golden after uncovering.

Nutritional Facts
Calories: 176 Kcal Proteins: 29 g Fats: 6 g Carbs: 24 g

3.33 Caesar salad cups

Prepping time: 5 mins, Cooking time: 12 mins, servings: 6

Ingredients

- 6 wonton wrappers
- 1 cup crushed romaine lettuce
- 1/4 cup crushed carrots
- 1 cup frozen, cooked chicken
- 2 tsp. bacon bits
- 2 tbsp. Caesar dressing
- 1 tbsp. crushed parmesan cheese

Directions

1. Set the oven to 350°f. Prepare a muffin tin of 6 cups using cooking spray.
2. Fill every muffin cup two-thirds of the way with a wonton wrapper and a wonton. Allow to cool for 8–12 mins after baking, or till golden brown.
3. Except for the parmesan cheese, mix all the ingredients in a mixing bowl and gently toss when you're ready to eat. Fill wonton cups half full of salad mix & top with cheese. Serve right away.

Nutritional Facts:

Calories: 190 Kcal Proteins: 24.3 g Fats: 4.3 g Carbs: 13 g

3.34 Mini crab cakes

Prepping time: 5 mins, Cooking time: 20 mins, servings: 18

Ingredients

- 2/3 cup Italian seasoning-flavored breadcrumbs
- 1/2 cup egg substitute
- 1/2 finely chopped bell pepper
- 1/2 chopped red onion
- 1 chopped rib celery
- 3 tbsp. light mayonnaise
- 2 tsp. lemon juice
- 1/2 tsp. salt
- 3/4 tsp. black pepper
- 1 tsp. crushed tarragon
- 3 cans of lump crabmeat
- 2 tbsp. vegetable oil

Directions

1. Except for the crabmeat and oil, put all the ingredients in a bowl and thoroughly mix. Fold these ingredients in crabmeat, taking care not to break the chunks.
2. Make 36 similar patties out from the mixture. Warm the oil in a big skillet on medium heat.
3. Batch-cook the patties for 2–3 mins, or until they are golden brown on both sides. Ideally, serve this dish when it's still warm.

Nutritional Facts
Calories: 201 Kcal Proteins: 32 g Fats: 10 g Carbs: 19 g

3.35 Cheesy mushroom flatbread

Prepping time: 10 mins, Cooking time: 5 mins, servings: 4

Ingredients

- 1 cup portobello mushrooms, sliced
- 3 tbsp. balsamic vinaigrette
- 1 roll-up of grain flatbread
- 1/3 cup crushed mozzarella cheese
- 1/4 tsp. garlic powder
- 1/8 tsp. black pepper

Directions

1. Set the oven to 450 °F. Use aluminum foil to line a cooking pan using cooking spray to coat the pan.
2. Mushrooms should be marinated for 10 mins in vinaigrette in a zip lock bag.
3. Place the flatbread in a baking pan. Add a layer of marinated mushroom on top and finish with a generous portion of garlic, pepper, & cheese.

4. The mushrooms should be soft, and the cheese should be melted in around 5-7 mins in the oven. Serve with quartered cutlets.

Nutritional Facts:
Calories: 192 Kcal Proteins: 27.6 g Fats: 4.5 g Carbs: 14 g

3.36 Mozzarella-asparagus roll-ups

Prepping time: 3 mins, cooking time: 10 mins, servings: 10

Ingredients

- 1/2 lb. asparagus spears
- 10 slices wheat bread
- 10 tsp. mayonnaise
- 1 tsp. garlic powder
- 5 sticks mozzarella cheese

Directions

1. Heat in advance the broiler. Prepare the baking sheet using cooking spray.
2. Using a medium-sized pan on high heat, bring 1 inch of water to boil. Cook the asparagus for 7-10 mins, depending on how soft you want your asparagus, and drain.
3. Every bread slice should be gently flattened using a rolling pin. On each side of the bread, spread 1 tbsp of mayonnaise. Garlic powder should be distributed evenly. Then add a few asparagus spears and cheese sticks on the top to finish it off. Cooking spray should coat the rolls before they are rolled up and placed on the baking sheet already prepared.
4. Broil for 5 mins at a distance of four to five inches from the heat source.

Nutritional Facts
Calories: 124 Kcal Proteins: 31 g Fats: 6 g Carbs: 14 g

3.37 Smoked salmon rounds

Prepping time: 5 mins, Cooking time: 5 mins, servings: 10

Ingredients

- 1 container cream cheese
- 1 sliced scallion
- 30 rounds melba toast
- 1 package smoked salmon
- 1 tbsp. red onion

Directions

1. Mix cream cheese and scallion in a mixing bowl until well-combined.

2. On the melba toast, apply the cream cheese mixture evenly. Sprinkle chopped onion on each and top with 1 slice of smoked salmon.

Nutritional Facts:
Calories: 165 Kcal Proteins: 30 g Fats: 12 g Carbs: 23 g

3.38 Healthy 7-layer dip

Prepping time: 5 mins, Cooking time: 5 mins, servings: 16

Ingredients

- 2 tbsp. canola oil
- 2 cans chickpeas
- 2 cloves garlic
- 6 tbsp. water
- 2 ripe avocados
- 1/4 tsp. salt
- 2 tbsp. lime juice
- 2 tomatoes
- 1/4 cup red onion, chopped
- 1 cup Greek yogurt
- 1/3 cup chopped cilantro
- 1 tsp. ground cumin
- 1/2 cup cheddar cheese
- 1/4 cup of black olives, sliced

Directions

1. On medium heat, warm oil in a pan till hot. Stir in the chickpeas and garlic for 5 mins, or till the chickpeas are gently browned.
2. Add boiling water to the chickpea mix and blend until smooth in a blender. Set aside a 10-inch circular serving dish on which to spread the mixture.
3. In a blender, combine avocado, salt, and lime juice, process till smooth. The mixture should be spread on the chickpea mix. Add the tomato and onion once you've finished sprinkling.
4. Toss the yogurt with cilantro, cumin, and salt in a small dish. On top of each of the veggies place a dollop of the mixture. Add cheese and olives. Place in refrigerator & keep chilled until you're ready to serve.

Nutritional Facts:
Calories: 187 Kcal Proteins: 21 g Fats: 8 g Carbs: 34 g

3.39 Speedy salmon croquettes

Prepping time: 10 mins, Cooking time: 28 mins, servings: 7

Ingredients

- 1 can of pink salmon
- 1 egg
- 2 tbsp. yellow mustard
- 2 tsp. chopped fresh parsley
- 1/2 tsp. onion powder
- 1/4 tsp. black pepper

- 3/4 cup stuffing mix
- 1/2 cup flour
- 1/4 cup vegetable oil

Directions

1. Assemble the ingredients in a bowl and stir well. Form 14 tiny patties and place them on a baking sheet after mixing in the stuffing mix.
2. A shallow dish should be filled with flour for easy pouring. Make sure the salmon patties are well covered before adding them.
3. Heat a pan over medium-high heat and heat oil. Cook the patties in batches for about 2–3 mins, or till they are well-browned. Serve right away.

Nutritional Facts:
Calories: 210 Kcal Proteins: 38 g Fats: 12 g Carbs: 29 g

3.40 Cranberry-nut spread

Prepping time: 15 mins, Cooking time: 25 mins, servings: 15

Ingredients

- 1 package softened cream cheese
- 1/2 cup sweetened cranberries
- 2 tsp. orange peel
- 1/4 cup toasted walnuts, chopped

Directions

1. In a mixing bowl, blend all of the ingredients until well mixed. Serve after 30 mins in the refrigerator. Use tiny wholegrain crackers or celery as a side dish to go with it.

Nutritional Facts:
Calories: 187 Kcal Proteins: 37 g Fats: 9 g Carbs: 21 g

3.41 Veggie-stuffed mushrooms

Prepping time: 15 mins, Cooking time: 27 mins, servings: 6

Ingredients

- 12 mushrooms
- 1 tbsp. olive oil
- 1 shredded zucchini
- 1/2 chopped onion
- 1/2 chopped bell pepper
- 1/4 cup of breadcrumbs
- 1/2 tsp. garlic powder
- 1/4 tsp. salt
- 1/4 tsp. black pepper

Directions

2. Set oven at 350°F.
3. Finely cut fresh mushroom stems once they've been removed from the caps.
4. Put the oil at medium flame in a pan and heat it. Mix the zucchini, onion, and bell pepper with the mushroom stems. Cook all the ingredients for 5 minutes, or until the vegetables are tender. Mix the garlic powder, pepper, and salt with the breadcrumbs.
5. Place the stuffed mushroom caps on a large, ungreased baking sheet with a rim and fill each cap with the vegetable mix. The mushrooms should be cooked through and soft when you remove them from the oven, around 20-25 mins. Serve it right away.

Nutritional Facts:
Calories: 164 Kcal Proteins: 34 g Fats: 12 g Carbs: 34 g

3.42 Baked sesame shrimp

Prepping time: 10 mins, Cooking time: 15 mins, servings: 10

Ingredients

- 1 cup flour, self-rising
- 1/4 tsp. salt
- 1/4 tsp. red pepper powder
- 3/4 cup club soda
- 1 lb. medium shrimp
- 2 tsp. sesame seeds

Directions

1. Set the oven to 400°F. Spray cooking spray on baking sheets with a rim.
2. Mix the flour, pepper, and salt in a mixing bowl. Whisk in the club soda until well blended after adding it to the flour mix.
3. Using your hands, hold the shrimp by their tails and dip each of them in the batter till they are thoroughly covered. Spread out the shrimp on baking sheets in a single layer, approximately 3 inches apart.
4. After sprinkling with the sesame seeds, gently sprinkle cooking spray on each shrimp. Bake for 12-13 mins for best results, or till the top is a deep golden brown.

Nutritional Facts:
Calories: 165 Kcal Proteins: 28 g Fats: 8 g Carbs: 28 g

3.43 Cheesy artichoke dip

Prepping time: 5 mins, Cooking time: 15 mins, servings: 16

Ingredients

- 2 cans artichoke hearts, drained & chopped
- 1 can mild green chilies,
- 6 tbsp. mayonnaise
- 1 1/2 cup cheddar cheese

Directions

1. Heat the oven at 350°F and prepare the food. Using a nonstick cooking spray, grease a baking dish.
2. Except for 1/2 cup shredded cheddar cheese, put all ingredients in a bowl. Place in the baking dish and bake for 30 mins. The last of the cheese should be sprinkled over everything.
3. Make sure the mixture is bubbling & cooked thoroughly, around 15 mins in the oven.

Nutritional Facts:
Calories: 135 Kcal Proteins: 30 g Fats: 8 g Carbs: 13 g

3.44 Taco shrimp bites

Prepping time: 5 mins, Cooking time: 5 mins, servings: 8

Ingredients

- 3 tsp. chili powder
- 1/4 tsp. salt
- 24 raw shrimp
- 1 lime in from of juice
- 1 avocado
- 1/3 cup sour cream
- 1 tsp. cumin
- 2 tbsp. fresh cilantro, chopped
- 24 tortilla scoops

Directions

1. Set the oven at 375°F. Spray the baking sheet using nonstick cooking spray and set it aside.
2. Merge 1/8 teaspoon salt and chili powder in a large zip lock bag. Throw in the shrimp and continue tossing till uniformly coated. On the baking sheet, put the shrimp in a single layer. Add half of the lime juice and toss to combine. Allow to bake for approximately 5-8 mins, or till shrimp is pink all the way through and no longer opaque in the middle.
3. Toss the avocado with the leftover lime juice and salt in a bowl.
4. Pour sour cream into another dish and stir in 1 tbsp of cilantro.
5. Make an avocado-sour cream mix & spread it over each tortilla chip. Add shrimp on top. End up serving with the remaining cilantro on top.

Nutritional Facts
Calories: 135 Kcal Proteins: 29 g Fats: 8.4 g Carbs: 23.4 g

3.45 Sun-dried tomato pesto dip

Prepping time: 10 mins, Cooking time: 25 mins, servings: 16

Ingredients

- 2 packages softened cream cheese
- 1/2 cup parmesan cheese
- 1/3 cup light mayonnaise
- 2 tbsp. lemon juice
- 1 tsp. garlic powder
- 1/2 tsp. onion powder
- 1/2 cup chopped tomatoes, sun-dried
- 1/2 cup walnuts, toasted
- 1/3 cup packed basil leaves
- 1 tbsp. parmesan cheese

Directions

1. Set oven at 350°F and prepare the dish. Before preparing the pie filling spray a 9-inch pie pan with nonstick cooking spray
2. Prior to adding any ingredients, ensure to whisk cream cheese and 1/2 cup of parmesan cheese until thoroughly combined in the bowl.
3. Combine walnuts, basil and dried tomatoes in a food processor and pulse until finely chopped.
4. Spoon tomato mix into pie pan and top with cream cheese mixture. One more tbsp of parmesan cheese should be added on top.
5. To heat thoroughly, bake for 25-30 mins. Prepare and serve right away.

Nutritional Facts:
Calories: 224 Kcal Proteins: 39 g Fats: 12.2 g Carbs: 30.4 g

3.46 Baked jalapeno poppers

Prepping time: 10 mins, Cooking time: 30 mins, servings: 12

Ingredients

- 8 ounces softened cream cheese
- 1 cup cheddar cheese, shredded
- 1 tsp. garlic powder
- 2 eggs
- 2 tbsp. milk, reduced fat
- 1 cup panko bread crumbs
- 1/2 tsp. paprika
- 1/2 tsp. chili powder
- 1/2 tsp. salt
- 1/4 tsp. black pepper
- 12 jalapeno peppers

Directions

1. Heat the oven to 350°Fahrienhiet and prepare the food. Spray the baking sheet using nonstick cooking spray and set it aside.
2. Mix the cheddar cheese, cream cheese, and garlic powder in a bowl. Beat the eggs and milk both in a bowl. Mix breadcrumbs with chili powder, paprika, pepper, and salt in a clean bowl.
3. Fill the center of every jalapeño half with 1 tbsp of the cheese mixture. Dip one by one in egg mixture and then press it into breadcrumbs to coat it.
4. Bake for 30-35 mins, or till brown on the outside.

Nutritional Facts:
Calories: 204 Kcal Proteins: 36 g Fats: 10.4 g Carbs: 34.5 g

3.47 Crunchy blue cheese stuffers

Prepping time: 5 mins, Cooking time: 10 mins, servings: 6

Ingredients

- 4 washed and trimmed celery stalks
- 1/4 cup blue cheese
- 1 package cream cheese
- 1/4 tsp. cayenne pepper
- 1/2 tsp. onion powder
- 1/4 tsp. salt
- 1 1/2 tsp. milk, fat-free
- Paprika for seasoning

Directions

1. Cut the celery, each piece a third of an inch.
2. Then mix the ingredients in a bowl and stir until well-combined (about 2 mins). Add the milk and continue mixing until it's creamy. Sprinkle paprika over spooned-on celery, then toss to coat. Refrigerate or serve immediately.

Nutritional Facts:
Calories: 189 Kcal Proteins: 41 g Fats: 9.9 g Carbs: 13.9 g

3.48 Hot Diggity dog "bites"

Prepping time: 8 mins, Cooking time: 12 mins, servings: 16

Ingredients

- 1/4 cup yellow mustard
- 2 tbsp. pickle relish, sweet
- 8 flour tortillas
- 8 hot dogs
- Toothpicks

Directions

1. Heat the oven at 350°Fahrienhiet and prepare the food in the oven. Use cooking spray to grease a baking dish.
2. Incorporate the relish and mustard in a medium bowl and whisk to combine thoroughly. Distribute the mixture on the tortillas in an even layer.
3. Roll up each tortilla with a hot dog on edge. The tortillas' ends should be trimmed and thrown away. Using a toothpick, separate every roll into 8 equal pieces.
4. Bake hot dog bites for 12-15 mins, or till they are cooked through. Place them on the baking sheet.

Nutritional Facts:
Calories: 154 Kcal Proteins: 35 g Fats: 19 g Carbs: 27 g

3.49 Crunchy chicken nibblers

Prepping time: 10 mins, Cooking time: 25 mins, servings: 4

Ingredients

- 1 cup cornflake crumbs
- 1/2 cup pancake and baking mix
- 1/2 tsp. paprika
- 3/4 lb. boneless chicken breasts
- 1/2 tsp. garlic powder
- 1/2 tsp. salt
- 1/4 tsp. black pepper
- Cooking spray

Directions

1. Set the oven to 400°F. Sprinkle cooking spray on a baking pan and line with foil.
2. Mix baking mix, cornflake crumbs, garlic powder, paprika, pepper and salt to taste and put all ingredients in a big zip loc bag. In the bag, put the chicken pieces and shake them to cover. Place on a baking sheet that has been preheated to 350°F. Cook the chicken on a nonstick pan.
3. Place chicken in the oven for 12-15 mins, or till not pink. Prepare the food and serve it right away.

Nutritional Facts
Calories: 256 Kcal Proteins: 41 g Fats: 21 g Carbs: 8 g

3.50 Creamy fiesta bites

Prepping time: 15 mins, Cooking time: 30 mins, servings: 16

Ingredients

- 1 tub cream cheese
- 2 tbsp. salsa, non-chunky
- 2 1/2 tsp. chili powder
- 1/2 tsp. cumin
- 3 tbsp. green onions, chopped
- 8 warmed wheat tortillas, low carb
- 2 tbsp. chopped cilantro

Directions

1. Mix salsa, cream cheese, 2 tbsp of green onion, 2 tsp chili powder and cilantro in a mixing bowl. Top each hot tortilla with a quarter cup of the mixture and fold the sides in.
2. Tightly roll the filled tortillas and cut each one into four bite-size pieces. Toothpicks are useful for securing bites.
3. Cover and refrigerate for 30 mins. Garnish with ½ teaspoon of chili powder and 1 tbsp of green onions over a serving platter.

Nutritional Facts:
Calories: 135 Kcal Proteins: 24 g Fats: 9 g Carbs: 7 g

3.51 Teriyaki cocktail meatballs

Prepping time: 5 mins, Cooking time: 15 mins, servings: 10

Ingredients

- 1 lb. ground pork
- 1/3 cup chopped scallion
- 1 cup wheat bread crumbs
- 1/3 cup teriyaki marinade
- 1/2 tsp. black pepper

Directions

1. Set the oven to 400°F. Prepare a baking sheet with cooking spray. To line the baking sheet, use aluminum foil.
2. Pork, breadcrumbs, scallion, black pepper and 2 tbsp marinade should be mixed in a medium bowl. Make approximately 20 meatballs using the mixture, using two tbsp per meatball; place on the baking sheet. Apply the marinade using a brush.
3. Bake for 15-20 mins, or till no pink is left, basting a couple of times during baking.

Nutritional Facts:
Calories: 177 Kcal Proteins: 33 g Fats: 24 g Carbs: 7 g

3.52 Southern deviled eggs

Prepping time: 5 mins, Cooking time: 10 mins, servings: 12

Ingredients

- 6 boiled eggs
- 3 tbsp. light mayonnaise
- 1 tbsp. sweet pickle and patted dry relish
- 1 tbsp. Dijon mustard
- Paprika for seasoning

Directions

1. Take the egg yolks, mustard, mayonnaise, and relish in a small dish and whisk thoroughly.
2. Place halved eggs on the dish, then fill using yolk mixture. Cover with plastic wrap, then top additional paprika and chill until ready to be served.

Nutritional Facts:
Calories: 209 Kcal Proteins: 36 g Fats: 19 g Carbs: 20 g

3.53 Easy cucumber cups

Prepping time: 5 mins, Cooking time: 10 mins, servings: 8

Ingredients

- 2 big cucumbers
- 1 cup ham, cubed and cooked
- 3 boiled eggs
- 1/2 cup plain yogurt
- 1/4 cup mayonnaise
- 2 tbsp. Dijon mustard
- 1/4 cup dill and drained pickle relish
- 1/2 cup chopped scallion (reserve 1 tbsp for garnish)
- 1/4 tsp. black pepper

Directions

1. Take a partial scoop out of the middle of each cucumber slice, being careful about leaving the base of each slice unbroken.
2. Then add the egg mix and ham and blend well in the food processor. Combine the other ingredients and process until smooth.
3. Then spoon the ham mixture into the cucumber cups and top with the scallions you saved for garnish. Chill the mixture until ready to be served or serve immediately.

Nutritional Facts:
Calories: 188 Kcal Proteins: 13 g Fats: 0.8 g Carbs: 46 g

3.54 Italian style caponata

Prepping time: 10 mins, Cooking time: 30 mins, servings: 16

Ingredients

- 2 tbsp. vegetable oil
- 1 big unpeeled eggplant, chopped
- 1 chopped onion
- 2 tbsp. garlic powder
- 1/2 cup chopped green olives, pimiento-stuffed
- 3 chopped ribs celery
- 1 can tomato sauce
- 1/4 cup white vinegar

- 1/3 cup brown sugar

Directions

1. In the saucepan, heat the olive oil to a medium-high flame. Add the onion, eggplant, and garlic powder & cook for approximately 5 mins or till the eggplant softens, turning periodically.
2. Toss the other ingredients and simmer for 25 mins, occasionally stirring, for the flavors to meld together.
3. You may either serve it right away or cover it and wait for it to cool completely.

Nutritional Facts:
Calories: 186 Kcal Proteins: 14 g Fats: 5 g Carbs: 19 g

3.55 Bistro stuffed tomato bites

Prepping time: 10 mins, Cooking time: 10 mins, servings: 5

Ingredients

- 10 cherry tomatoes
- 1/2 cup cheese spread
- Parsley for garnish, chopped

Directions

1. Set a serving dish with the tomato halves over top of it.
2. Fill each tomato half with roughly a tsp of cheese. Serve immediately, or chill till ready to be served. Garnish fresh parsley on it before eating.

Nutritional Facts:
Calories: 184 Kcal Proteins: 35 g Fats: 20 g Carbs: 12 g

3.56 Zesty sausage meatballs

Prepping time: 7 mins, Cooking time: 15 mins, servings: 12

Ingredients

- 1 lb. ground pork
- 1/2 cup breadcrumbs
- 1/4 cup water
- 1 chopped onion
- 1/4 cup chopped parsley
- 1 tsp. fennel seed, crushed
- 1/2 tsp. garlic powder
- 1/4 tsp. red pepper powder
- 1/2 tsp. salt
- 1/2 tsp. black pepper

Directions:

1. Heat the oven at 350°Farhienhiet and prepare the food in the oven. Spray a baking sheet by using oil and set aside. Combine all the ingredients and thoroughly mix them in a large bowl. Make 36 balls of one inch out of the mixture.
2. Flip meatballs once midway through baking and bake for an additional 15-18 mins, or no longer pink.
3. Broil for 2-3 mins at a distance of 4 to 5 inches from the heat source, just until the top is golden brown. Prepare and serve right away.

Nutritional Facts:
Calories: 213 Kcal Proteins: 38 g Fats: 14 g Carbs: 24 g

3.57 Hot 'n' crispy zucchini bites

Prepping time: 5 mins, Cooking time: 10 mins, servings: 6

Ingredients

- 2 zucchinis
- 1/2 cup breadcrumbs
- 1 tbsp. parmesan cheese
- 1 tbsp. mayonnaise
- 1/2 tsp. garlic powder
- 1/2 tsp. onion powder
- 1/4 tsp. seasoned salt
- 1/4 tsp. black pepper

Directions

1. Prepare the oven for broiling by preheating it to high heat. To cover a baking sheet, use aluminum foil.
2. Bring 1 inch of water to boil in a medium saucepan at high heat. Lower the heat, and cook the zucchini slices for 3-5 mins, or until they are soft. To soak up the water, use paper towels and pat dry.
3. Add cheese, onion powder, salt, garlic powder, black pepper, and toss in breadcrumbs; stir until well-combined. On every side of the zucchini, slice, spread mayonnaise & coat it by using breadcrumbs. Place the coated side on the lined baking sheet.
4. Cook them for 2 to 3 mins or till golden brown; set to 4 to 5 inches from the fire. Prepare the food and serve it right away.

Nutritional Facts:
Calories: 138 Kcal Proteins: 32 g Fats: 8 g Carbs: 21 g

3.58 Chicken & Vegetable Penne with Parsley-Walnut Pesto

Prepping time: 20 mins, Cooking Time: 10 mins, Serving: 4

Ingredients

- ¾ cup chopped walnuts
- 1 cup parsley leaves
- 2 cloves crushed garlic
- ½ tsp. plus 1/8 tsp. of salt
- ⅛ tsp. ground pepper
- 2 tbsp. olive oil

- ⅓ cup Parmesan cheese
- 1 ½ cups shredded cooked chicken breast
- 6 ounces fusilli pasta
- 8 ounces green beans
- 2 cups cauliflower florets

Directions
1. A big pot of the water should be brought to a rolling boil.
2. Put walnuts in a microwave-safe bowl and heat on high for 2 1/2 to 3 mins, or till scented and lightly toasted. Set aside to cool on a plate. Keep 14 cups for sprinkling over salads and other dishes.
3. Then, combine the remaining half-cup of walnuts with parsley, salt, pepper, and garlic in a food processor. Process the nuts to a fine powder. While the processor is working, add a small amount of oil gradually into the food processor. Pulse the Parmesan until well-combined. Make a big bowl of pesto by scraping it up with a spatula. Include chicken in the mix.
4. Boil the pasta for 4 mins, then drain. Stir in cauliflower and green beans, cover, and cook for an additional 5-7 mins, just until pasta is almost tender, but not quite. To warm the pesto-chicken mix, remove 3/4 cup of cooking liquid and mix it into the mixture before draining.
5. Add vegetables and pasta to pesto-chicken mix after they have been drained. Toss everything together until it's well-coated. Each serving should be divided evenly among 4 pasta bowls, with 1 tbsp of the reserved chopped walnuts on top of each bowl.

Nutritional Facts
Calories: 514 Kcal, Protein: 31.4 g, Carb: 43.3 g, Fat: 26.6 g

3.59 Spinach, Apple & Chicken Salad with Poppy Seed Dressing & Cheese Crisps

Prepping time: 20 mins, Cooking Time: 20 mins, Serving: 4

Ingredients
- 3 sheets phyllo pastry
- 4 tsp. olive oil
- 1 beaten egg white
- ⅓ cup Parmigiano-Reggiano cheese
- 1 tbsp. thyme leaves
- 3 tbsp. buttermilk
- 2 tbsp. honey
- 1 tbsp. cider vinegar
- 1 tsp. poppy seeds
- ½ tsp. Dijon mustard
- ½ tsp. kosher salt
- 5 cups baby spinach
- 1 ½ cups shredded cooked breast chicken
- 1 sliced Gala apple

Directions:
6. Preheat the oven to 350°F. Utilize the parchment paper to line the baking sheet.
7. Lay out a phyllo sheet on the baking sheet you just prepared. Apply 2 tbsp of oil to the hair and let it air dry. Gently press to adhere the 2nd sheet phyllo on top. 2 tbsp of oil brushed on. Brush the egg white on the third sheet before placing it on top. Add cheese and thyme to the dish and mix well. Trim the phyllo pile into 2" squares with a sharp knife. Bake them for 8 mins or until golden brown. Allow standing for about three mins before using.

8. Make a medium bowl and mix the remaining 2 tbsp of oil, honey, buttermilk, and vinegar with the remaining poppy seeds and the mustard and salt.
9. Place chicken, spinach, and apple in a large bowl. Toss to combine.
10. Plate and enjoy! Make phyllo crisps and serve them alongside the entree.

Nutritional Facts
Calories: 349 Kcal, Protein: 23.1 g, Carb: 26.1 g, Fat: 16.7 g

3.60 Hazelnut-Parsley Roast Tilapia

Prepping time: 20 mins, Cooking Time: 10 mins, Serving: 4

Ingredient:
- 2 tbsp. olive oil
- 4 tilapia fillets
- ⅓ cup chopped hazelnuts
- ¼ cup chopped parsley
- 1 small shallot
- 2 tsp. lemon zest
- ⅛ tsp. salt
- ¼ tsp. ground pepper
- 1 ½ tbsp. lemon juice

Directions
1. Preheat the oven to 450°F. Brush 1 tbsp of oil on a rimmed baking sheet; line with foil. Prepare fish by letting it sit out counter for 15 mins to bring it to room temperature.
2. While that's happening, in a small bowl, combine the toasted parsley, hazelnuts, shallot, 1 tbsp oil, lemon zest, pepper & 1/8 teaspoon salt.
3. Pat the fish dry on both sides using a paper towel. Prepare a baking sheet with nonstick spray and lay out the fish on it. Lemon juice and the leftover 2 teaspoons of oil should be applied to the fish's surface on both sides. Sprinkle the remaining 1/8 tsp pepper and 1/4 tsp salt on both sides evenly. Pat gently to adhere the hazelnut mixture to the top of the fillets after dividing it evenly among them. Roast the fish for 7-10 mins till it is firm, opaque, and flaky. Serve right away.

Nutritional Facts
Calories: 262 Kcal, Protein: 30.2 g, Carb: 3.3 g, Fat: 15 g

3.61 Charred Vegetable & Bean Tostadas with Lime Crema

Prepping time: 25 mins, Cooking Time: 30 mins, Serving: 6

Ingredients

Lime Crema
- 5 tbsp. sour cream
- ⅛ tsp. lime zest
- 2 tsp. lime juice
- ⅛ tsp. kosher salt

Tostadas

- 6 corn tortillas
- 2 tbsp. canola oil
- 4 sliced cloves garlic
- 1 ½ tsp. ground cumin
- 1 tsp. kosher salt
- ⅛ tsp. chipotle pepper powder
- 2 cans black beans
- ¼ cup water, and more if necessary
- 2 sliced red bell chili
- 1 sliced red onion
- 2 zucchinis
- 1 cup fresh or frozen corn kernels
- ¼ tsp. ground pepper
- 1 cup shredded cabbage
- ¼ cup chopped cilantro
- 6 tbsp. crumbled cotija

Directions

1. Get the crema ready by following these steps: In a mixing bowl, mix lime zest, sour cream, lime juice, and salt. Place on the back burner.
2. Prepare the tostadas: set the oven at 400°F. Place a rack in the upper third of the oven.
3. Brush 1 tbsp of oil on both sides of the tortillas and organize on a baking tray. If they overlap slightly, that's fine. They'll shrink in size as they cook. Bake for 10 mins, tossing once halfway through. Cool completely on a wire rack.
4. Now in a large skillet, heat 2 tbsp of oil over medium heat. Stir in 1 clove of garlic and cook for 30 seconds until fragrant. Toss in the cumin, 1/2 tsp salt and the chili powder, and cook for 30 seconds while stirring. Stir in the beans and cook for 4 mins, frequently stirring, until heated through. Add 1/4 cup of water to the beans in the food processor and process until smooth. Pulse till smooth, adding 1 tbsp. Add water if necessary; do not over-process.
5. Turn the oven's broiler to high and preheat it.
6. A large bowl is ideal for mixing all of the ingredients before cooking. Cook all of the ingredients together in a large skillet over medium-high heat until softened but not mushy. Spread over a large baking sheet with a rim you can see through the middle. Broil for 8 to 12 mins, occasionally stirring, till lightly charred.
7. Place a few tostadas on each plate and top with some of the beans and the rest of the ingredients, charred vegetables, cilantro, shredded cabbage, cheese, & any remaining crema.

Nutritional Facts
Calories: 327 Kcal, Protein: 13.1 g, Carb: 43.3 g, Fat: 12.5 g

3.62 Chicken Enchilada Skillet Casserole

Prepping time: 15 mins, Cooking Time: 25 mins, Serving: 6

Ingredients

- 2 tbsp. olive oil
- 1 cup corn kernels
- ½ cup green diced bell pepper
- ½ cup red diced bell pepper
- ½ cup diced onion
- 1 package baby spinach
- 2 ½ cups shredded cooked chicken breast
- 1 pouch red enchilada sauce
- 1 ¼ cups prepared salsa
- 8 corn tortillas

- 1 ½ cups shredded cheddar cheese
- 1 cup grape tomatoes, chopped
- ¼ cup fresh cilantro, chopped
- ¼ cup radishes, matchstick-cut

Directions
1. Preheat the oven to 350°F before beginning.
2. In the ovenproof frying pan, heat oil over moderate flame until hot. Add the corn, green and red peppers, and onion. Cook and stir, for 7-10 mins, until charred. Spinach can be added in small batches and cooked for about one and a half mins, stirring constantly.
3. Combine the enchilada sauce, chicken, and salsa. Toss in the tortilla strips with a spatula. Add a little cheese to finish it off. Bake for 15 mins till bubbly after being transferred to the oven.
4. Add cilantro, tomatoes, and radishes to the top of the casserole.

Nutritional Facts
Calories: 342 Kcal, Protein: 30 g, Carb: 25 g, Fat: 14 g

3.63 Low-Carb Cauliflower Fried Rice with Shrimp

Prepping time: 10 mins, Cooking Time: 20 mins, Serving: 4

Ingredients
- 2 tbsp. chicken broth, unsalted
- 2 tbsp. soy sauce, reduced sodium
- 3 tsp. chili-garlic sauce
- 8 oz. big shrimp
- 2 tbsp. vegetable oil
- 1 tbsp. minced garlic
- 1 tbsp. minced ginger
- 1 cup caps of shiitake mushroom
- ½ cup diced carrots
- 1 1-lb. package of riced cauliflower
- 1 cup shelled edamame, frozen
- 3 tbsp. fresh cilantro, chopped

Directions
1. In a mixing bowl, mix soy sauce, broth, and hot-garlic sauce for taste. Cut shrimp into 1/2-inch pieces and pat dry till thoroughly dried.
2. If you're using a 12-inch stainless-steel skillet, heat till one drop of the water vaporizes within 1–2 seconds after contact is made with the flat bottom of the pan. Add 1 tbsp of oil and mix well. Stir in the ginger and garlic with a metal spatula for approximately 10 seconds, just until the ginger is barely aromatic. Depending on how pink the shrimp are, drying for a min or two is the best way to prepare it. Place on a platter and serve.
3. Add the tbsp of oil and mix well. Sautee the vegetables for one min once they have been added. Remove and save 14 cup broth mixture; stir in cauliflower, edamame, and remaining 14 cup broth mixture. Cook for one min with the lid on, on high heat. For 1 min, remove the lid and stir-fry the shrimp and veggies for 1 min more or when the shrimp is just cooked through. Add a few sprigs of cilantro for flavor.

Nutritional Facts
Calories: 219 Kcal, Protein: 14 g, Carb: 19 g, Fat: 10 g

3.64 Lemon Chicken & Rice

Prepping time: 25 mins, Cooking Time: 1 hour 20 mins, Serving: 8

Ingredients
- 2 tbsp. olive oil
- 8 boneless chicken thighs
- 2 thinly sliced onions
- ½ tsp. salt
- 3 cloves garlic
- 2 tsp. ground turmeric
- 1 tsp. paprika
- 1 pinch of a generous pinch of saffron
- 3 cups shredded cabbage
- 4 cups brown rice, cooked
- ¼ cup lemon juice
- 2 tbsp. chopped Italian parsley
- 1 sliced lemon

Directions
1. Set the oven to 375°F. Brush cooking spray on two 8-inch baking dishes and foil pans.
2. Over moderate heat, heat 1 tbsp oil in a non-stick frying pan. Cook the 4 chicken thighs for approximately 4 mins on each side, rotating once. Set the chicken aside on a platter when you've finished cooking it. Make a second batch of thighs by repeating the process with the leftover chicken. Except for 1 tbsp Remove all the fat from the pan.
3. Add the onions and 1/4 teaspoon salt to the pan with the leftover 1 tbsp oil. Toss until golden and tender, about 12-15 mins. Cook for 2 mins while adding in the turmeric, garlic, paprika, and saffron, if using. Place the onions on a platter and put them away for later.
4. Add the cabbage to the pan and bring it back to moderate heat. Stirring often, cook for 3 mins or until wilted. Reserving half of the onion, add the lemon juice, rice, and 1/4 teaspoon salt to the dish. Cook for a further 5-7 mins, or when rice is tender and the sauce has thickened.
5. Place 4 of the saved chicken thighs for each prepared baking pan, then top each with a generous portion of the rice mixture. Place half of the leftover sautéed onions on top of each serving. Use aluminum foil to shield both dishes from the elements. One should be labeled and kept frozen for up to a month before eating.
6. For the last 30 mins of baking, place the covered dish in the oven.
7. Turn oven off, remove the cover, and bake an additional 5 to 10 mins, or until the chicken is done and a thermometer inserted into the widest part of the thigh reads 165°F. Sprinkle with lemon slices and parsley, if desired.

Nutritional Facts
Calories: 274 Kcal, Protein: 17 g, Carb: 30 g, Fat: 10 g

3.65 Pumpkin Seed Salmon with Maple-Spice Carrots

Prepping time: 15 mins, Cooking Time: 30 mins, Serving: 4

Ingredients
- 4 fresh salmon fillets
- 1 lb. carrots
- ¼ cup maple syrup
- ½ tsp. salt

- ½ tsp. pumpkin pie spice
- 8 crushed saltine crackers
- 3 tbsp. chopped salted, roasted pumpkin seeds (pepitas) plus 2 teaspoons, divided
- Cooking spray

Directions
1. If the fish was frozen, thaw it first. Set the oven to 425°F. Prepare a baking pan by lining it with aluminum foil and storing it.
2. Combine carrots with 3 tbsp maple syrup, 1/4 teaspoon salt, and pumpkin spice in a large mixing bowl. Bake the carrots in the prepared pan, spreading them out to cover the bottom half of the pan. Ten mins in the oven should be enough.
3. The fish should be rinsed and dried with towels while you wait. Combine the smashed crackers with the leftover pumpkin seeds and 1/4 tablespoon of salt on a small plate. Use the leftover 1 tbsp of maple syrup to glaze the fish. Press the cracker mixture into the cheese to help it stick. Bake the fish with the vegetables in the baking dish. Cooking spray all fish lightly on the topside. Fork-tender fish and carrots are achieved by baking for an additional 10-15 mins.
4. Serve the carrots with the leftover two tablespoons of pumpkin seeds, dividing them between dinner plates. Add the smoked salmon on top and serve.

Nutritional Facts
Calories: 359 Kcal, Protein: 28 g, Carb: 30 g, Fat: 14 g

3.66 Salmon Couscous Salad

Prepping time: 10 mins, Cooking Time: 5 mins, Serving: 1

Ingredients
- ¼ cup cremini mushrooms, sliced
- ¼ cup diced eggplant
- 3 cups baby spinach
- 2 tbsp. vinaigrette
- ¼ cup Israeli couscous, cooked
- 4 oz. cooked salmon
- ¼ cup sliced apricots
- 2 tbsp. goat cheese, crumbled

Directions
1. Heat a small skillet to moderate flame and spray with cooking spray. Add the mushrooms and eggplants; simmer, occasionally turning, for 3-5 mins, or till gently browned as well as the juices are released. Set aside after being removed from the heat. On a plate, combine spinach and 1 tbsp and 1 tsp vinaigrette; toss well to combine.
2. Place the couscous on top of spinach & toss with the leftover 2 tablespoons of vinaigrette. Add the fish to the dish and serve. Adding dried apricots and goat cheese to the sautéed veggies will finish it off perfectly!

Nutritional Facts
Calories: 464 Kcal, Protein: 35 g, Carb: 35 g, Fat: 22 g

3.67 Vegan Cauliflower Fettuccine Alfredo with Kale

Prepping time: 15 mins, Cooking Time: 30 mins, Serving: 6

Ingredients
- ½ cup toasted breadcrumbs
- 1 tbsp. fresh parsley, chopped
- ½ tsp. lemon zest
- 4 cups cauliflower florets
- 1 cup raw cashews
- 8 oz. fettuccine
- 4 cups sliced kale
- 3 tbsp. lemon juice
- 2 tbsp. white miso
- 2 tsp. garlic powder
- 2 tsp. onion powder
- ¾ tsp. salt
- 1 cup water

Directions
1. Heat a big kettle of water.
2. In a mixing bowl, combine parsley, breadcrumbs, and lemon zest.
3. Serve with cashews or cauliflower. Boil the cauliflower and cashews together for 15 mins or until the cauliflower is soft. Transfer the cauliflower and cashews to a mixer with a slotted spoon.
4. Then, add the spaghetti and simmer for about 10 mins, tossing it around. Cook for a further 1 min, stirring in the greens, before serving. Remove the spaghetti and greens from the heat and put them back in the saucepan.
5. Blend the miso, lemon juice, garlic powder, salt, onion powder, and 1 cup of water till smooth. Stir the spaghetti in the sauce until that is fully coated. Serve with a sprinkling of breadcrumbs on top.

Nutritional Facts
Calories: 325 Kcal, Protein: 12 g, Carb: 47 g, Fat: 11 g

3.68 Curried Sweet Potato & Peanut Soup

Prepping time: 10 mins, Cooking Time: 40 mins, Serving: 6

Ingredients
- 2 tbsp. canola oil
- 1 ½ cups yellow onion
- 1 tbsp. minced garlic
- 1 tbsp. minced ginger
- 4 tbsp. curry paste
- 1 serrano chili
- 1 lb. sweet potatoes
- 3 cups water
- 1 cup coconut milk
- ¾ cup roasted peanuts
- 1 can rinse white beans
- ¾ tbsp. salt
- ¼ tbsp. ground pepper
- ¼ cup chopped cilantro
- 2 tbsp. lime juice
- ¼ cup pumpkin seeds, roasted
- Lime wedges

Directions
1. Heat oil on a big saucepan on medium heat. Cook the onion for approximately 4 mins, often turning, until tender and transparent.

2. Make a sauce by combining coconut milk, curry paste, and sriracha sauce. Bring them to boil, then add the sweet potatoes and water. Reduce the heat and cook the sweet potatoes for 10 to 12 mins with the lid partly on.
3. Blend 1/2 of soup with coconut milk and peanuts until smooth. Add the remaining soup to the pot and heat through. Bring all the boil and then remove from heat. Add beans, pepper and salt to taste. Take the heat off and let sit for a few mins. Add the cilantro and the lime juice and mix well. Incorporate the pumpkin seeds & lime juice into the dressing and serve with the wedges.

Nutritional Facts
Calories: 345 Kcal, Protein: 13 g, Carb: 38 g, Fat: 19 g

3.69 Spinach & Strawberry Salad with Poppy Seed Dressing

Prepping time: 15 mins, Cooking Time: 20 mins, Serving: 4

Ingredients
- 2 ½ tbsp. mayonnaise
- 1 ½ tbsp. cider vinegar
- 1 tbsp. olive oil
- 1 tsp. poppy seeds
- 1 tsp. sugar
- ¼ tsp. salt
- ¼ tsp. ground pepper
- 1 package baby spinach
- 1 cup sliced strawberries
- ¼ cup sliced almonds, toasted

Directions
1. A big bowl is the best place to combine the mayonnaise with the other ingredients. Add the spinach and the strawberries, tossing to coat. Add some sliced almonds for crunch.

Nutritional Facts
Calories: 154 Kcal, Protein: 3 g, Carb: 7 g, Fat: 13 g

3.70 Chicken & Cucumber Lettuce Wraps with Peanut Sauce

Prepping time: 10 mins, Cooking Time: 30 mins, Serving: 4

Ingredients
- ¼ cup peanut butter, creamy
- 2 tbsp. soy sauce
- 2 tbsp. honey
- 2 tbsp. water
- 2 tsp. sesame oil, toasted
- 2 tsp. olive oil
- 3 scallions, sliced and separated
- 1 serrano minced pepper
- 1 tbsp. minced ginger
- 2 tsp. minced garlic
- 1 lb. ground chicken
- 1 cup diced jicama
- 16 Bibb lettuce leaves
- 1 cup rice, cooked brown

- 1 cup English cucumber, sliced
- ½ cup cilantro leaves
- For serving, lime wedges

Directions
1. In a mixing bowl, mix soy sauce, peanut butter, honey, sesame oil and water.
2. In a nonstick skillet, warm olive oil over moderate flame. Toss in serrano peppers, scallion whites, ginger, and garlic, then sauté for 2 minutes or softened. Add the chicken and simmer for 3-4 mins, smashing it up with a potato masher as it cooks.
3. Stir in the peanut sauce and boil for 3 mins, just until the sauce gets thickened. Take it off the heat. Add the jicama and scallion greens and mix well to combine.
4. Make eight stacks of two lettuce leaves each for serving. Place rice in each lettuce cup. Top with the cucumber, chicken mixture, and cilantro if used. Serving suggestions: squeeze fresh lime juice over each plate.

Nutritional Facts
Calories: 521 Kcal, Protein: 34 g, Carb: 44 g, Fat: 26 g

3.71 Tofu & Snow Pea Stir-Fry with Peanut Sauce

Prepping time: 15 mins, Cooking Time: 15 mins, Serving: 4

Ingredients
- ⅓ cup peanut butter, unsalted
- 3 tbsp. rice vinegar
- 2 tbsp. soy sauce
- 2 tsp. brown sugar
- 2 tsp. hot sauce
- 1 package firm tofu
- 4 tsp. canola oil
- 1 package frozen pepper vegetables, stir-fry
- 2 tbsp. chopped ginger
- 3 cloves garlic
- 2 cups trimmed snow peas
- 2 tbsp. water
- 4 tbsp. roasted peanuts, unsalted
- 2 cups brown rice, cooked

Directions
1. Mix vinegar, peanut butter, soy sauce, spicy sauce, and sugar until smooth.
2. Drain the tofu, then pat dry with such a piece of paper. Cut it into 3/4-inch pieces, then pat dry another time.
3. over a moderate flame, heat a large nonstick skillet with 2 tbsp of oil. Stir in half of the tofu and cook, uncovered, for 2 mins, or until it's just beginning to brown on the bottom. Cook, stirring periodically, for 1-2 mins or until well-browned all over. Place on a platter and serve. Repeat with the remaining tofu and 1 tbsp—oil in the pan.
4. Add the last 1 tbsp of oil to the pan and heat through. Toss in frozen veggies with ginger and garlic, and cook for 2-3 mins, or until the vegetables are thawed and aromatic. Add the snow peas and mix well. Cook for 3-4 mins till the peas become crisp-tender after adding water and covering.
5. Move the veggies to the pans outside the borders to prevent them from sticking. Stir in the saved peanut sauce for the last 30 seconds of cooking time. Put the veggies to the sauce and mix well. Stir in tofu that was set aside and cook for 30-60 seconds, depending on how firm you want your tofu. To

produce a creamy sauce, if required, add additional water. Serve with 1 tbsp of peanuts on top of each dish and a side of rice.

Nutritional Facts
Calories: 514 Kcal, Protein: 23 g, Carb: 49 g, Fat: 26 g

3.72 Chicken & Sun-Dried Tomato Orzo

Prepping time: 05 mins, Cooking Time: 35 mins, Serving: 4

Ingredients

- 8 oz. orzo
- 1 cup water
- 1/2 cup chopped tomatoes
- 1 plum tomato
- 1 clove garlic
- 3 tsp. chopped marjoram
- 1 tbsp. vinegar
- 2 tsp. and 1 tbsp. olive oil, separated
- 4 breasts of boneless chicken
- ¼ tsp. salt
- ¼ tsp. ground pepper
- 1 package artichoke hearts, frozen
- ½ cup Romano cheese

Direction

1. Prepare orzo in a large pot of boiling water according to package instructions for 8-10 mins or until just tender. Rinse and drain well.
2. Meanwhile, combine 1/4 cup tomatoes, 1 cup water, garlic, 1 plum tomato and 2 tsp. oil, then also add 2 tsp. marjoram and vinegar into a blender. Blend until there are just a few clumps left.
3. On all sides, season the chicken using pepper & salt. In a large frying pan, heat leftover 1 tbsp oil over medium-high heat. Add chicken and cook it for 3-5 mins on each side, regulating the heat, if necessary, to prevent scorching. To keep it warm, place it on a platter and cover it with foil to prevent spillage.
4. Boil tomato sauce, then pour it into the pan. Take 1/2 cup of the sauce and put it in a small bowl. Add the orzo, artichoke hearts, and 6 tbsp of cheese to the pan, including the leftover 1/4 cup tomatoes. Cook for 1-2 mins, often stirring, until well cooked. Distribute the mixture among the four plates.
5. Cut the chicken into thin slices. Combine leftover cheese and marjoram in a small bowl and serve over pasta with 2 tbsp of the leftover tomato sauce.

Nutritional Facts
Calories: 456 Kcal, Protein: 36 g, Carb: 54 g, Fat: 12 g

3.73 Easy Pea & Spinach Carbonara

Prepping time: 05 mins, Cooking Time: 15 mins, Serving: 4

Ingredients

- 1 ½ tbsp. olive oil
- ½ cup panko breadcrumbs
- 1 clove garlic
- 8 tbsp. Parmesan cheese
- 3 tbsp. chopped parsley
- 3 egg yolks

- 1 large egg
- ½ tsp. ground pepper
- ¼ tsp. salt
- 1 package fresh tagliatelle
- 8 cups baby spinach
- 1 cup peas

Directions
1. In a pot on the stovetop, bring 10 cups of water to a boil.
2. A big skillet with moderate flame should have oil in it. Cook, tossing regularly, until toasted, approximately 2 mins, adding breadcrumbs and garlic as needed. Add 2 tbsp of parmesan and parsley to the small bowl with the pasta & toss to coat. Separate yourself from the situation.
3. combine the egg yolks, pepper, and salt with the other 6 tbsp of parmesan in a medium bowl.
4. While boiling, cook pasta for one min while tossing it. Cook for another min, stirring in spinach & peas. 14 cups of water should be saved. Place in a wide basin after draining.
5. Whisk the egg mix slowly while adding the conserved cooking water. Toss the spaghetti with tongs while you gradually pour the sauce mix. Reserve a little of the breadcrumb mixture and serve the soup with it.

Nutritional Facts
Calories: 430 Kcal, Protein: 20 g, Carb: 51 g, Fat: 15 g

3.74 Sweet Potato-Black Bean Burgers

Prepping time: 15 mins, Cooking Time: 30 mins, Serving: 4

Ingredients
- 2 cups sweet potato
- ½ cup rolled oats
- 1 cup black beans
- ½ cup chopped scallions
- ¼ cup vegan mayonnaise
- 1 tbsp. tomato paste
- 1 tsp. curry powder
- ⅛ tsp. salt
- 1/2 cup almond milk yogurt
- 2 tbsp. chopped fresh dill
- 2 tbsp. lemon juice
- 2 tbsp. olive oil
- 4 toasted hamburger buns
- 1 cup sliced cucumber

Directions
1. Place shredded sweet potato in a wide dish and squeeze dry with towels. Add the ground oats to bowl with both sweet potatoes after processing in the blender till finely ground. Use your hands to smash the mix together after adding the beans & scallions, tomato paste, mayo, curry powder, and salt. Form into 4 patties. Refrigerate the patties for 30 mins after placing them on a platter.
2. In a small dish, combine yogurt, dill, and lemon juice; leave aside.
3. Medium heat a big cast-iron skillet with the oil. Add patties and cook for 3 mins on each side or till golden brown.
4. Make a yogurt sauce and divide it evenly between the upper and bottom buns. Replace the top bread halves after placing a burger on each bottom half and slicing cucumber on top for garnish.

Nutritional Facts
Calories: 454 Kcal, Protein: 12 g, Carb: 54 g, Fat: 22 g

3.75 Curried Chickpea Stew

Prepping time: 20 mins, Cooking Time: 40 mins, Serving: 8

Ingredients
- 1 bag prewashed spinach
- 1 ½ tbsp. canola oil
- 1 chopped large onion
- 1 piece fresh ginger
- ½ to 1 chopped jalapeño pepper
- 3 cloves garlic
- 1 tbsp. curry powder
- 3 thinly sliced carrots
- ½ head cauliflower
- 2 cans chickpeas, rinsed
- 2 cans diced tomatoes
- ⅓ cup coconut milk

Directions
1. Add 1 tbsp water and 1 tbsp spinach to a microwave dish; cover. Stirring periodically, cook on high for 1-2 mins, or until barely wilted. Drain in a colander after transferring to it. Squeeze out all the remaining water after it's cold enough to handle. Set aside the coarsely chopped ingredients.
2. Cook oil in a pan Dutch oven/nonstick pan with high edges. Stir, add onion and simmer for 8 mins or until transparent. Stir in jalapeno, ginger, garlic, and curry powder for about 30 seconds, remove from the heat, and let cool slightly. Add carrots and 2 tbsp of water; cover and simmer for approximately 10 mins, stir periodically. Add the cauliflower, and simmer for 5-10 mins, turning periodically, until just tender-crisp.
3. Stir in half-and-half tomatoes and coconut milk. Bring to the boil, but don't let it scorch. Simmer for about 15 mins, covered on low heat with occasional shaking. Reserving the spinach (or other greens) until the end, warm it thoroughly.
4. Label and store the remaining half of the mix (approximately 5 cups) in a 1 1/2-quart freezer container for roughly a month. The leftover half may be served right once or stored in the refrigerator for up to three days.

Nutritional Facts
Calories: 430 Kcal, Protein: 20 g, Carb: 51 g, Fat: 15 g

3.76 Pork & Green Chile Stew

Prepping time: 25 mins, Cooking Time: 4 hours, Serving: 6

Ingredients
- 2 lb. boneless shoulder roast
- 1 tbsp. vegetable oil
- ½ cup chopped onion
- 4 cups cubed potatoes
- 3 cups water
- 1 can hominy
- 2 cans chili peppers
- 2 tbsp. cooking tapioca
- 1 tsp. garlic salt
- ½ tsp. ground cumin
- ½ tsp. ancho powder chili
- ½ tsp. ground pepper
- ¼ tsp. dried oregano
- 1 tbsp. chopped cilantro

Directions
1. Remove any visible fat from the meat. Make 1/2-inch-wide cuts in the meat. Cook 1/2 of meat till browned in oil in a pan over medium-high flame. Take the meat out of the pan with a slotted spoon, and place it on a plate. Cook the leftover meat and onion in the same manner. Remove the fat by squeezing it out. In a 3- to a 4-quart slow cooker, combine the beef and onion.
2. Combine all ingredients in a large saucepan and bring it to boil on low heat and simmer for 30 mins. Add the potatoes and oregano towards the end. Cover and simmer about 7-8 hours on low or 4-5 hours on high, depending on your preference. Add a sprinkling of chopped cilantro to each plate if desired.

Nutritional Facts
Calories: 180 Kcal, Protein: 15 g, Carb: 23 g, Fat: 5 g

3.77 Trapanese Pesto Pasta & Zoodles with Salmon

Prepping time: 15 mins, Cooking Time: 20 mins, Serving: 6

Ingredients
- 2 zucchinis
- 1 tsp. salt
- ½ cup raw almonds
- 1 lb. grape tomatoes
- 1 cup basil leaves
- 4 cloves garlic
- ¼ tsp. red pepper, crushed
- 3 tbsp. olive oil
- 8 oz. spaghetti
- 1 lb. salmon fillets
- ¼ tsp. ground pepper
- 2 tbsp. Parmesan cheese

Directions
1. Boil water in a large pot. Utilize a vegetable peeler or spiralizer to make long, small slices of zucchini. Set colander over a big dish to catch the juices. Allow draining for 15-20 mins after adding 1/4 teaspoon of salt.
2. Then, in a blender, roughly chop almonds till crumbly. Pulse in the tomatoes, garlic, 1 cup of basil leaves, and red pepper flakes till roughly chopped. Add the rest of the garlic and the basil leaves. Then, blend in 2 tbsp extra-virgin olive oil and 1/2 teaspoon salt until mixed.
3. In a pot of boiling water, cook the pasta according to the package directions, until al dente. Discard the liquid, and then pour it all into a big mixing basin. Zucchini should be squeezed carefully to remove any extra water before being added to the pasta.
4. In a large pan, heat the leftover 1 tbsp of oil till shimmering. Use 1/4 teaspoon salt and pepper to season the fish. Cook salmon for approximately 4 mins on the bottom, until it's brown and crispy. Cook salmon for a further 2-4 mins, or when it flakes when tested with a fork. Use a spoon to gently separate the meat on a platter once you've transferred it.
5. Toss in the pesto with the spaghetti and coat well. Add the salmon and mix well. Add the last ¼ cup of chopped fresh basil on top. Add more pepper and parmesan if needed.

Nutritional Facts
Calories: 450 Kcal, Protein: 30 g, Carb: 40g, Fat: 6 g

3.78 Maple-Roasted Chicken Thighs with Sweet Potato Wedges and Brussels Sprouts

Prepping time: 20 mins, Cooking Time: 50 mins, Serving: 4

Ingredients

- 2 tbsp. maple syrup
- 4 tsp. olive oil
- 1 tbsp. Snipped thyme
- ½ tsp. salt
- ½ tsp. black pepper
- 1 lb. sweet potatoes
- 1 lb. Brussels sprouts
- Cooking spray
- 4 bone-in skinned chicken thighs
- 3 tbsp. snipped cranberries
- 3 tbsp. chopped pecans

Directions
1. Set the oven to 425°F. Add 1/4 teaspoon of pepper and salt to a small bowl and whisk in maple syrup, thyme, oil, and 1 tsp oil. Sweet potatoes and Brussels sprouts should be combined in a big dish. With 1 tbsp of residual oil, the other 1/4 teaspoon salt, and the other 1/4 tsp pepper, coat the vegetables and serve.
2. Prepare a 15-by-10-inch baking pan by lining it with aluminum foil. Let it sit for 5 mins in the preheated oven. Using cooking spray, spray the pan after removing it from the oven. Place the chicken in the pan, fleshy side up. Place the chicken in the center of the plate and surround it with the veggies. Cook for 15 mins in a hot oven.
3. Brush the chicken and veggies with the maple syrup mix after they have been turned over. Roast for an additional 15 mins, or until the chicken is cooked through and the potatoes are fork tender. Serve with cranberries and pecans for garnish.

Nutritional Facts
Calories: 436 Kcal, Protein: 34 g, Carb: 45 g, Fat: 15 g

3.79 Jambalaya Stuffed Peppers

Prepping time: 20 mins, Cooking Time: 40 mins, Serving: 6

Ingredients

- 6 bell peppers
- 1 ½ lb. boneless chicken thighs
- 2 tbsp. Cajun seasoning
- 2 tbsp. olive oil
- 1 andouille sausage
- ½ cup celery
- 1 onion
- 2 cloves garlic
- ½ tsp. salt
- 1 can tomatoes
- ¼ cup tomato paste
- 1 cup chicken broth
- 1 cup brown rice, uncooked

Directions

1. Preheat the oven to 400°F. Line a baking sheet with such a rim with aluminium foil or parchment paper.
2. Removing the core and seeds from peppers requires cutting the tops off the peppers and being extremely cautious not to fracture the skin. Set aside the pepper caps after dicing them. Bake the peppers for 20 mins on the preheated baking sheet. Take it out of the oven, and then let it cool for a while Drain any liquid that has gathered at the bottom.
3. Meanwhile, rub 1 tbsp Cajun spice all over the chicken. On low heat, fry the bacon in 1 tbsp of oil until crisp and golden-brown. Cook for 4-6 mins with half of the chicken, flipping to brown both sides. Scoop the chicken into a medium bowl and set aside. Toss in one more tablespoon of olive oil and the rest of the chicken and cook until the chicken is done.
4. Cook the sausage in the pan for 1-2 mins, turning periodically. Then, sauté for 3-5 mins until transparent, often turning the onion, celery, and saved chopped pepper. Keep stirring for about 30 seconds until the garlic is fragrant. Add the rest of the Cajun spice and salt. Using a rubber spatula, scrape off any browned parts from the bottom of the bowl, add tomatoes and tomato paste. Bring the broth to a boil. Add the rice and chicken, along with any collected liquids. Bring the mixture to a rolling boil. Cook, tossing periodically until the chicken is cooked through or the rice is mushy, 5-10 mins after reducing the heat to a simmer.
5. Removing the pan from the heat then stirring it will do the trick. To serve, spoon ¼ cup of the chicken mix through each pepper and mound it on top if required. Let rest, covered, for 10 mins to allow liquid to soak. Bake for approximately 20 mins, or until well warmed through.

Nutritional Facts
Calories: 346 Kcal, Protein: 30 g, Carb: 31 g, Fat: 11 g

3.80 Ginger Beef Stir-Fry with Peppers

Prepping time: 10 mins, Cooking Time: 30 mins, Serving: 4

Ingredients

- 12 oz. flank steak
- 1 ½ tbsp. cornstarch
- 1 tbsp. soy sauce
- 1 tbsp. dry sherry
- 1 tbsp. vegetable oil
- 4 tbsp. hoisin sauce
- 4 tbsp. ketchup
- 1-3 tbsp. chili-garlic sauce
- 3 peeled gingers, sliced
- 1 yellow onion
- 1 cup bell pepper, green
- 1 cup bell pepper, red
- 2 tbsp. beef broth

Directions

1. Make the thin slices of the meat against the grain. Slice every strip of fabric into pieces by cutting it against the grain. Stir until there is barely any visible cornstarch in a medium bowl. Combine 1 and 1/2 tsp soy sauce, beef, and 1 tsp sherry. Stir in 1 tsp oil as well as the steak until it is just coated.
2. Add remaining 1 and 1/2 tsp of soy sauce and 1 tbsp sherry to the hoisin sauce, ketchup, and garlic sauce to taste.
3. If you're using a stainless-steel pan, heat it until a drop of the water evaporates in about 1 to 2 seconds after it comes into contact. Add the last tablespoon of oil and mix well. Stir in ginger, then cook for 10

seconds to release its flavor. Move ginger to a side of the grill and add the meat, being sure to distribute it evenly around the pan. Cook for approximately 1 min, occasionally stirring, until the meat is beginning to brown. Add the onion and stir-fry for 30 seconds to 1 min, using only a metal spatula, till the meat is golden brown but not fully done. On a platter, combine the meat and onions and serve.

4. Toss in the chopped green and red peppers, as well as some chicken stock, to the pan. Cover & cook the peppers for approximately a min until they are brilliant green & red with practically no liquid remaining, around high heat. Replenish the meat mixture in the pan, along with any collected juices. Stir in the leftover sauce, then heat for 30 seconds to 1 min, depending on the thickness of the meat and the tenderness of the peppers. If preferred, discard the ginger.

Nutritional Facts
Calories: 215 Kcal, Protein: 20 g, Carb: 11 g, Fat: 10 g

3.81 Pork Skewers with Fruit Glaze

Prepping time: 10 mins, Cooking Time: 30 mins, Serving: 6

Ingredients
- 1 egg
- ⅓ cup water chestnuts, chopped
- ¼ cup dry breadcrumbs
- 2 tsp. fresh ginger
- 1 clove garlic
- ¼ tsp. salt
- ¼ tsp. ground pepper
- 1 lb. pork loin
- 1 bell pepper
- ⅔ cup fruit preserves
- ¼ cup pineapple juice
- 1 tbsp. lemon juice
- ¼ tsp. ground cardamom

Directions
1. Combine the water chestnuts, egg, and breadcrumbs with ginger and garlic, and season with salt and pepper. Add the ground pork and thoroughly combine. Make 30 meatballs using the pork mix.
2. Leave half an inch between each piece of meatball and bell pepper when you thread skewers and put them aside.
3. Put fruit preserves in a shallow dish and remove any big pieces before making the glaze. Add the lemon, pineapple and cardamom juices, then mix well. Bring the juice to the boil and then turn down the heat to a simmer. Cook for 15 mins with the lid off. While pork is cooking, place the pan on the counter to cool for about 10 mins.
4. Prepare a drip pan and moderate coals for the charcoal grill. Above the pan, make sure the heat is set to medium. Oil the grill rack and place it on the pan with the skewers. Turn off the grill and then let the meatballs sit for about 10-12 mins, or until they lose their pink color, and thus the liquids flow clear. Apply a thin layer of fruit glaze using a brush. Do not wait to take skewers off the grill; do it immediately. Preheat a gas grill. Reducing the temperature to medium-low is a good idea. Cook as described above.
5. Continue to serve skewers with glaze.

Nutritional Facts
Calories: 187 Kcal, Protein: 19 g, Carb: 18 g, Fat: 4 g

3.82 Red Cabbage-Apple Cauliflower Gnocchi

Prepping time: 15 mins, Cooking Time: 15 mins, Serving: 4

Ingredients
- 3 cups red cabbage
- 2 tbsp. water
- 1 tbsp. olive oil
- 1 bag cauliflower gnocchi, frozen
- ½ cup unsweetened applesauce
- 1 tbsp. Dijon mustard
- ground pepper for taste

Directions
1. Put the cabbage in a big baking dish and cook it according to the package directions. Add 1 tbsp of water in it then cover and microwave on "High" until softened for about 5 mins..
2. Medium heat a big skillet with the oil. Cook the gnocchi for approximately 5 mins, often tossing, until golden. Cover and simmer the cabbage for a few mins, stirring regularly, until the water has evaporated. Add applesauce, mustard, then salt and pepper to taste. Add a little pepper to your food to give it some more flavor.

Nutritional Facts
Calories: 153 Kcal, Protein: 2 g, Carb: 21 g, Fat: 1 g

3.83 Chicken-Spaghetti Squash Bake

Prepping time: 30 mins, Cooking Time: 60 mins, Serving: 8

Ingredients
- 1 spaghetti squash
- 4 cups broccoli florets
- 1 tbsp. canola oil
- 1 package sliced mushrooms
- 1 chopped onion
- 2 cloves garlic
- ½ tsp. dried thyme
- ½ tsp. ground pepper
- 2 cans mushroom soup with condensed cream
- 1 ½ lb. boneless chicken breasts
- ½ cup cheddar cheese

Directions
1. Set the oven to 375°F. Spray 2 8-inch baking plates with nonstick cooking spray and place in the oven to bake for 30 mins.
2. Cut the squash in half longitudinally and remove the seeds with a spoon. Add 2 tbsp of water to the dish and place the cut-side down a chicken. For 10-12 mins on high, heat the meat until it could be scraped off with a spoon, but it is still soft. Gather all the strands together, place them in a bowl.
3. Cover the broccoli with 1 tbsp of water and microwave on high for 1 min. Stirring periodically, cook on high for 2-3 mins, or until slightly soft. Set aside to chill after draining.

4. A big nonstick pan over moderate flame is a good place to start heating the oil. Cook the mushrooms for approximately 8 mins, often stirring, until they have released their juices. After that, add the onion and simmer for another 8 mins, or until the onion is soft & the mushrooms are gently browned.
5. Add the thyme, garlic, and pepper, and simmer for 30 seconds while stirring. Add the soup and heat it through without diluting it with water. Add the squash, chicken, and broccoli, and gently mix to incorporate.
6. Distribute the mix among prepared baking plates and top with ¼ cup of the Cheddar cheese on everyone. Wrap the foil with plastic wrap to keep it from leaking. One casserole may be labeled and frozen, lasting to 1 month.
7. Bake the rest of the casserole for approximately 25 mins till it begins to bubble. Remove the lid and bake for an additional 10-15 mins, or until the edges are just beginning to brown. Serve after 10 mins of letting it stand.

Nutritional Facts
Calories: 273 Kcal, Protein: 25g, Carb: 11 g, Fat: 18 g

3.84 Vegetarian Stuffed Cabbage

Prepping time: 30 mins, Cooking Time: 1 hour 30 mins, Serving: 4

Ingredients
- 1 cup water
- ½ cup brown rice
- 1 tsp. olive oil
- 1 Savoy cabbage
- 1 lb. Bella mushrooms
- 1 chopped onion
- 4 cloves garlic
- ½ tsp. rubbed sage
- ½ tsp. crumbled rosemary
- 1/2 tsp. salt
- 1/4 tsp. ground pepper
- ½ cup red wine
- ¼ cup currants
- 1/3 cup pine nuts, chopped and toasted
- 2 tbsp. olive oil
- 1 chopped onion
- 1 garlic
- ¼ tsp. salt
- ¼ tsp. ground pepper
- 1 can crushed tomatoes

Directions
1. Bring a small pot of water, rice, and 1 tsp of oil to boil. Turn down the heat to a low simmer, cover, and cook for 40-50 mins, or when the water has been drained and the rice is soft. Place in a big bowl and put away until needed.
2. Boil a pot of water. Place a cooking sheet close to the fire, lined with a dry dishtowel.
3. Scrape the center of the cabbage out from the bottom using a small, serrated knife. Cook cabbage for about 5 mins in hot water, after which insert the kale. To extract the huge outer leaves, wait for the leaves to soften before carefully removing them with tongs. Place the leaves on a baking sheet & blot them dry with extra paper towels. Separate yourself from the situation.
4. For several mins, rinse and drain the leftover cabbage. About 3 cups of chopped vegetables should be finely chopped. You may use up the rest of the cabbage in another recipe.
5. In a large pan, heat 1 ½ teaspoons of oil on moderate flame. In a large skillet over medium-high heat, combine the butter and oil; cook, occasionally turning, for 8-10 mins or until onions are translucent

and the pan is almost dry. Cook for a further 3 mins, occasionally stirring, before adding the wine. Stir in the currants, cooked rice, & pine nuts when the mix has been cooled.
6. In a medium-sized pan, heat 1/2 tbsp of oil until shimmering. Cook, occasionally tossing, till the cabbage becomes wilted and begins to brown, 3-5 mins, adding the additional 1/4 tsp salt & 1/8 tsp pepper. Add this to the rice mix to give it some flavor.
7. To make the sauce, follow these steps: Heat 1 tbsp oil over a moderate flame in a large frying pan. Toss in the vegetables and heat them for 2 to 4 mins, often turning, until the onion and garlic soften. Bring tomatoes and wine to a boil and cook for approximately 10 mins, or until considerably thickened.
8. Set the oven to 375°F.
9. Stuffing a cabbage requires the following steps: Cut away the thick stem in the middle of a spare cabbage leaf but leave the leaf whole. In the middle, distribute approximately 3/4 cup of the filling. Make a fold in the middle and place the filling in the middle. Fill the other 7 leaves, and after that, repeat the process with the rest of the filling.
10. In a baking dish, pour 1 cup of tomato sauce. Then, with the seam face down, place the filled cabbage rolls over the top of the sauce. Add the rest sauce and 1 tbsp of oil to the rolls and toss to combine.
11. Bake uncovered for 45 mins, baste with sauce.

Nutritional Facts
Calories: 544 Kcal, Protein: 15 g, Carb: 60 g, Fat: 24 g

3.85 Pesto Shrimp Pasta

Prepping time: 10 mins, Cooking Time: 30 mins, Serving: 4

Ingredients
- 1 cup dried orzo
- 4 tsp. pesto sauce
- 2 tbsp. olive oil
- 1 lb. medium shrimp
- 1 zucchini
- ⅛ tsp. coarse salt
- ⅛ tsp. cracked pepper
- 1 lemon
- 1 oz. Parmesan cheese

Directions
1. Preparation of orzo pasta should be done following the instructions on the box. Before draining reserve 3 tbsp of pasta water. With a fork, mix 1 tsp of pesto mixture with the cooking water you've saved and save.
2. Combine 3 tbps of the pesto mixture with 1 tbsp of olive oil in a big zip-lock bag while the pasta is cooking to make the sauce. To blend, place the lid on the bag and give it a good shake. Seal the bag and spin the shrimp to coat them with the coating before securing the bag.
3. Stirring often, cook the zucchini for 1-2 mins in remaining 1 tbsp heated oil in a large pan on medium-high heat. The pesto-marinated shrimp should be cooked for 4-5 mins, depending on how opaque you want your shrimp to be.
4. Toss the spaghetti with the shrimp, Zucchini, and lemon juice in the skillet. Stir in the pasta water, scraping up any browned bits from the bottom as you go until it's all absorbed. Add a pinch of kosher salt and freshly ground black pepper to taste. Well, before serving, squish the lemon pieces over the

spaghetti and toss them around. Add a flutter of cheese made with cheddar of shredded Parmesan cheese and serve.

Nutritional Facts
Calories: 361 Kcal, Protein: 32 g, Carb: 36 g, Fat: 10 g

Chapter 4: Breakfast Recipes

4.1 Scallion Grits with Shrimp

Prepping time: 15 mins, Cooking Time: 20 mins, Servings: 6

Ingredients

- 1 ½ cups milk, fat-free
- 1 ½ cups water
- 2 bay leaves
- 1 cup corn grits, stone-ground
- ¼ cup seafood broth
- 2 minced garlic cloves
- 2 scallions, green and white parts
- 1 lb. shrimp
- ½ tsp. dried dill
- ½ tsp. smoked paprika
- ¼ tsp. celery seeds

Directions

1. Bring the milk, bay leaves and water to boil in a large stockpot at high heat.
2. Stir constantly as you add grits in little amounts at a time.
3. Cover and continue cooking at low heat the grits for about 5-7 mins, occasionally stirring, until grits become soft and mushy. When done cooking, remove bay leaves and toss them in the trash.

4. Take broth to just a simmer in a pan over low heat.
5. Fry scallions & garlic for 3-5 mins, depending on how tender you want your garlic & scallions.
6. Toss in the shrimp, paprika, celery seeds & dill, and cook for 7 mins, or unless it becomes pink all the way through but not overdone.
7. Add a quarter cup of grits to each serving plate, then top with a few shrimps.

Nutritional Facts:

Calories: 197 Kcal, Proteins: 20 g, Fats: 1 g, Carbs: 25 g,

4.2 Flourless Savory Cheddar Zucchini Muffins

Prepping time: 10 mins, Cooking Time: 25 mins, Servings: 8

Ingredients

- 1¼ cup almond flour
- 3 eggs
- ½ tsp. baking soda
- ¼ tsp. coarse salt*
- ¼ tsp. black pepper
- ½ tsp. onion powder
- ½ tsp. garlic powder
- 1 cup plus 1 tbsp. grated cheddar cheese
- 1 cup grated and squeezed zucchini

Directions

1. Set oven to 350°F.
2. In the blender, combine the dry ingredients and baking soda, spices, and eggs. Add zucchini and one cup of cheese. Once the zucchini is uniformly mixed, pulse the hand blender until it's done. There should still be little specks of green visible in the batter at this point.
3. Fill the muffin pan 3/4 full of the batter. Add the 1 tbsp. of cheese on top if desired. Bake for 25 mins at 350°F or until brown and a toothpick when inserted comes out clean.
4. Take out the muffins from the pan and place them on a wire rack to finish cooling for 3 to 5 mins, or until they are cold enough even to touch. Ideally, serve this dish when it's still warm.

Nutritional Facts:

Calories: 196 Kcal Proteins: 15 g Fats: 10 g Carbs: 5 g

4.3 Mini Corn, Cheese and Basil Frittatas

Prepping time: 10 Mins, Cooking Time: 33 Mins, Servings: 8

Ingredients

- Spray for cooking
- 2 tbsp. ghee
- 1 cup chopped onion
- 10 eggs

- 1 cup grated Gruyere cheese
- ¾ cup whole milk
- ¼ tsp sea salt
- ¼ tsp paprika
- 1 cup corn kernels
- 1 cup thin-sliced basil leaves

Direction:
1. Heat the oven at 350°F and prepare the oven. Set aside a 12-cup muffin pan sprayed with nonstick cooking spray.
2. A big frying pan with one tbsp. of ghee should be heated up first. Sauté the onion for five mins at the moderate flame, or until transparent. Add some garlic and cook for an additional 2 mins. Allow cooling after removing from heat.
3. Then, in a clean bowl, beat the eggs until they are light and fluffy. Whisk in the cheese, milk, paprika, corn, and basil after you've added the other ingredients. Microwave about 20 seconds with the last spoonful of butter inside a heatproof vessel. Ensure that you include all the flour in the egg mix before stirring it in. Whisk in the cooled onions after adding them to the egg mixture.
4. When using a muffin tin, fill each well approximately three-quarters full of the egg mix. Bake the devilled eggs for 28 mins or until golden brown and firm to the touch on top.
5. Before serving, allow the food to cool somewhat. For about 3 days in the refrigerator, they may be prepared ahead of time, chilled, and kept in a sealed container. It can be stored in the freezer for 3 months.

Nutritional Facts:
Calories: 180 Kcal Proteins: 18 g Fats: 12 g Carbs: 25 g

4.4 No-Bake Blueberry Almond Energy Snacks

Prepping time: 10 mins, Cooking Time: 10 mins, Servings: 10

Ingredients

- ⅔ cup raw almonds, finely chopped
- ⅓ cup blueberries, dried
- 1 ¼ cups old-fashioned oats
- ½ cup almond butter
- ¼ cup honey
- ¼ tsp. salt (optional but recommended)

Direction:
1. In a mixing bowl, whisk together all ingredients until well combined, about 3 minutes.
2. Scoop the contents into individual servings using a spoon. Bake on the baking sheet, rolling into balls with your hands.
3. Tip: wet your hands before rolling the material into a ball so it doesn't cling to your fingertips.
4. Refrigerate the balls for approximately an hour to allow them to harden. Keep in the refrigerator for up to 1 week in a sealed jar (but don't hold your breath).

Nutritional Facts:
Calories: 102 Kcal Proteins: 2 g Fats: 5 g Carbs: 10 g

4.5 Healthy Bagel Toppings, 4 ways

Prepping time: 15 mins, Cooking Time: 10 mins, Servings: 2

Ingredient

For the eggs and sausage bagels:

- 2 wheat bagels whole
- 3 eggs
- ¼ cup of grated mozzarella cheese
- 2 chicken sausages breakfast
- Salt & black pepper

For the spinach and mushroom bagels:

- 2 wheat bagels whole
- 1 tsp of olive oil
- 2 cups of fresh spinach
- 4 oz. of white sliced button mushroom
- 2 eggs
- Salt & black pepper

For the cream cheese and berries bagels:

- 2 wheat bagels whole
- 2 oz. of Cream cheese
- Assorted berries: blueberries, strawberries, blackberries
- A little amount of honey

For the peanut butter and banana bagels:

- 2 wheat bagels whole
- 3 tbsp of peanut butter
- 1 small, sliced banana
- Chia seeds (sprinkle of)
- A small amount of honey

Directions

For the egg and sausage bagels:

1. Bagels should be toasted.
2. A nonstick spray for cooking should be used in the pan that has been preheated on low heat.
3. In the bowl, crack the eggs and whisk them together using a fork till they are well mixed. Whisk in a little amount of water, salt, and pepper to taste.
4. Pour the eggs into the pan and cook them, stirring periodically, over low heat unless they are set. When the eggs are about to done, add the cheese and mix everything. Use pepper and salt to taste.

5. cook chicken sausages in a pan on medium heat, occasionally stirring, until cooked through and lightly browned. Slice after removing to a chopping board. Once the eggs are almost cooked, you may heat them in that pan with the eggs. To free up space, just push them to one side.

6. Add cheesy fried eggs and sausage to each side of the bagel. Serve the food while it's still hot.

For the spinach and mushroom bagels:

1. Bagels should be toasted.
2. In a large pan, preheat the olive oil over medium heat. Sauté the mushrooms until they've lost most of their liquid and then remove them from the heat. Squeeze lemon juice over the spinach mixture. Add pepper and salt to taste. Add spinach and cook, often stirring, until wilted to your desired consistency.
3. Dispose of the vegetables and break the eggs into skillet. Cooking spray or additional olive oil or butter, if preferred, may be used to prevent sticking. Fry the eggs to the desired doneness, about a min or two.
4. To cook the tops, you may choose to turn the burgers over. If you want to cook the tops quicker, you may cover the pan with a lid. Toss the chicken with a little salt and pepper, and then serve.
5. Place a fried egg on top of the mushrooms and spinach on each side of the bagel. Serve immediately, using pepper and salt to taste.

For the cream cheese and berries bagels:

1. Bagels should be toasted.
2. Top every bagel half with a thin layer of cream cheese. Spread honey over the berries before serving.

For the peanut butter and banana bagels:

1. Bagels should be toasted.
2. On each side of the bagel, spread a thin layer of peanut butter. Drizzle with chia seeds and honey before adding banana slices on top.

Nutritional Facts:
Calories: 160 Kcal Proteins: 15 g Fats: 18 g Carbs: 26 g

4.6 Mushroom Freezer Breakfast Burritos

Prepping time: 10 mins, Cooking Time: 20 mins, Servings: 4

Ingredients

- 2 tbsp. canola, grapeseed or vegetable oil
- ½ onion
- 2 minced garlic cloves
- 2 cups chopped mushrooms
- 4 cups chopped spinach
- ¼ tsp. salt
- 8 eggs
- 1 cup milk

- Pepper and salt
- Cooking spray
- 4 wheat tortillas
- ¼ cup plus 2 tbsp. goat cheese

Directions
1. In a pan, heat the oil over medium-high heat. Make sure to sauté the garlic and onion for a couple of mins to make sure they're transparent.
2. Continue to fry until lightly browned, approximately 2 mins more (about 3-4 mins). To ensure that the other side of the mushrooms is cooked, turn them over. Cook the spinach for 3-4 mins or until wilted in the pan. Add salt and combine the vegetables in a large bowl. Set aside once the heat has been removed.
3. In a bowl, whisk the milk and eggs together. Sprinkle with kosher salt and freshly ground black pepper, if desired.
4. Another big skillet should be heated at a medium-high temperature. Add the egg mix to the skillet after it has been sprayed with spray. Stir regularly for the last 4-5 mins of cooking time or until the eggs are set. Put the pan off from the heat and allow it to cool fully.
5. Microwave the tortillas for 10 seconds to warm them up. Spread 1 1/2 tbsp of cheese on all the tortillas before arranging them on four separate sheets of aluminum foil. Spread the roasted veggies and the scrambled eggs evenly among the four taco shells. Place each one in a bag in the freezer once it has been rolled up in foil. Freeze.
6. Unpack tortillas of foil when you're ready to eat them straight from the freezer. To cook evenly, place in a microwave-safe dish and heat on medium for 1-2 mins.

Nutritional Facts:
Calories: 385 Kcal Proteins: 20 g Fats: 22 g Carbs: 28 g

4.7 Vegetarian Lentils with Toasted Egg Recipe

Prepping time: 05 mins, Cooking Time: 10 mins, Servings: 4

Ingredients
- 2 oz. vegetable broth
- 2 onions, diced
- 2 minced garlic cloves
- ½ yellow pepper, sliced
- ½ pepper red, sliced
- ½ orange bell pepper, sliced
- 1 can lentils
- ½ tsp. smoked paprika
- ⅛ tsp. chipotle powder
- ½ tsp. garlic powder
- Black pepper to taste
- Olive-oil spray
- 2 eggs
- 2 slices bread
- 2 tbsp. parsley
- ¼ sliced avocado
- ½ sliced lemon

Directions
1. Cook garlic and onions in the vegetable broth in a broad sauté pan unless they become transparent, stirring periodically.

2. Toss the bell peppers and cook for a further 3-4 minutes, or until tender. Garnish with chopped cilantro. Add lentils and all the other ingredients to the sauce.
3. Continue to cook, stirring regularly, for a further 3-4 mins on medium heat. Make holes in each slice of bread with a plain-edge tiny circular cutter while you toast it.
4. Cook the sunny side of the eggs up in a medium skillet coated with oil.
5. On each dish, put a piece of bread with a hole over the yolk and top with an egg.
6. To serve, spread parsley over the top of every dish before adding lemon & avocado slices as garnishes. Squeeze a lemon over the lentil mixture, then sprinkle with salt and pepper.

Nutritional Facts:
Calories: 420 Kcal Proteins: 25 g Fats: 10 g Carbs: 62 g

4.8 High Protein Oatmeal

Cooking Time: 5 mins, Prepping time: 2 mins, Servings: 2

Ingredients

- 3/4 cup rolled oats
- 2 eggs
- 1/2 cup milk
- 1 tbsp. ground flaxseed
- 1 tsp. cinnamon
- 1 ripe mashed banana

Directions

1. To cook, combine all ingredients in a large saucepan over medium-high heat.
7. Cook, constantly stirring, until the oatmeal mix achieves a regular smoothness and eggs are not watery. Should take approximately five mins to complete.

Nutritional Facts:
Calories: 100 Kcal Proteins: 10 g Fats: 6 g Carbs: 12 g

4.9 Whole Wheat Blueberry Muffins

Cooking Time: 20 mins, Prepping time: 5 mins, Servings: 4

Ingredients

- 2 cups fresh or frozen blueberries
- 3 cups plus 1 tbsp. wheat flour
- 1 tbsp. baking powder
- ½ tsp. baking soda
- 10 tbsp. softened butter
- ¾ cup sugar
- 2 eggs
- 1 tsp. vanilla extract

- 1 tsp. lemon zest
- 1½ cups plain yogurt

Directions
1. Arrange the oven rack in the oven's middle, about halfway down. 375°F is the ideal temperature for baking. You may either oil every muffin cup separately or use paper liners in the ordinary muffin pan. Place on the back burner.
2. Toss blueberries with 1 tbsp. flour in a small bowl. Place on the back burner.
3. Combine the baking soda, flour, and baking powder in a separate basin. Place on the back burner.
4. Beat butter and sugar in a large dish until frothy. Each time you add an egg, make sure to beat it until it's well-integrated before adding the next. Add lemon zest and vanilla, combine well.
5. Be careful to whisk the ingredients unless combined in this step. Do not put too much pressure on yourself. Only about a third of dry ingredients should be added at this point. A third of the yogurt (about 125 ml) should be beaten in. Half of the leftover dry ingredients should be beaten in at this point. Add a third more of the yogurt and mix well. Next, add the rest of the dry ingredients and yogurt, and beat until combined. Include the berries in the batter by folding them in with a spatula.
6. Fill the muffin cups about 3-quarters full of the muffin dough for larger muffins and about two-thirds full for smaller muffins, using an ice cream scoop to divide the dough evenly among the cups.
7. When a toothpick put in the middle of one of the muffins comes out clean, it's done baking.

Nutritional Facts:
Calories: 98 Kcal Proteins: 12 g Fats: 8 g Carbs: 4 g

4.10 Mixed Berry Smoothie

Cooking Time: 5 mins, Prepping time: 5 mins, Servings: 2

Ingredients
- 1 cup yogurt, strained
- 1 cup berries or cherries, frozen
- 1 tbsp. sweetener
- 2 tbsp. nonfat milk or juice of any fruit (cranberry, pomegranate, cherry)

Instruction
1. To combine all ingredients, use an immersion blender. Continue processing until the mixture is smooth.

Nutritional Facts
Calories: 123 Kcal Proteins: 22 g Fats: 3 g Carbs: 30 g

4.11 Quinoa Breakfast Bowl

Prepping time: 5 mins, Cooking Time: 15 mins, Servings: 4

Ingredients
- 2 cups coconut milk
- 1 cup rinsed quinoa
- Optional: cinnamon powder, brown sugar, sugar replacement, honey, raisins, diced apple, chia seeds, vanilla yogurt, mint leaves and fresh blueberries.

Directions
1. Over a moderate flame, heat milk to an active boil, stirring often. Toss in some quinoa for extra protein and fiber. Boil for about 12-15 mins, covered, over low heat until liquid absorbed. Remove it from the heat and fluff using a fork until well-combined and fluffy. Add extra items to taste, if desired.

Nutritional Facts:
Calories: 217 Kcal Proteins: 10 g Fats: 5 g Carbs: 33 g

4.12 Whole Grain Banana Pancakes

Cooking Time: 20 mins, Prepping time: 10 mins, Servings: 8

Ingredients
- 1 cup wheat flour
- 1 cup all-purpose flour
- 4 tsp. baking powder
- 1 tsp. ground cinnamon
- 1/2 tsp. salt
- 2 eggs
- 2 cups milk, fat-free
- 2/3 cup banana
- 1 tbsp. olive oil
- 1 tbsp. maple syrup
- 1/2 tsp. vanilla extract
- Sliced bananas and additional syrup (if necessary)

Directions
1. To begin, combine the first five ingredients in a large bowl using a fork. Combine the milk, eggs, banana puree, oil, and 1 tbsp in a separate dish. of the syrup with the vanilla extract. Mix to the flour mix and whisk until wet, just a few seconds.
2. Prepare a skillet by spraying it with spray and heating it medium heat. Fill skillet with 1/4 cup butter at a time and heat until bubbles appear on the surface and edges are golden brown, about 1-2 mins each side. Turn the pan over and cook until the second side is golden brown. Sliced bananas and more maple syrup are optional garnishes.
3. Freeze cooled pancakes in a jar between sheets of waxed paper. Then reheat covered with aluminum foil in the preheated 375°F oven for 10-15 mins or until cooked, depending on the thickness of the pancakes. Alternatively, microwave a two-pancake stack on a microwave-safe dish for 45-60 seconds on high, until cooked through.

Nutritional Facts:
Calories: 186 Kcal Proteins: 7 g Fats: 4 g Carbs: 32 g

4.13 Hawaiian Hash

Cooking Time: 15 mins, Prepping time: 20 mins, Servings: 6

Ingredients
- 2 tsp. canola oil
- 1 tsp. sesame oil
- 4 cups sweet potatoes, peeled
- 1 cup onion
- 1/2 cup red pepper, chopped
- 1 tsp. ginger root, minced
- 1/4 cup water
- 1 cup cooked ham, cubed
- 1 cup fresh pineapple
- 1/4 cup salsa Verde
- 1 tsp. soy sauce
- 1/2 tsp. sesame seeds, black
- Chopped cilantro
- Macadamia nuts, chopped

Directions
1. Heat all the oils in a pan over medium heat. Cook and stir for 5 mins with the onions, sweet potatoes, pepper, onion, and ginger root. To this, add a little liquid. Cook the potatoes for 8-10 minutes at low heat, stirring once or twice throughout cooking.
2. Stir in the remaining 5 ingredients and cook, often stirring, for 2 mins on a moderate flame, or until well cooked. Serve with crushed cilantro and chopped macadamia nuts, if preferred.

Nutritional Facts
Calories: 158 Kcal Proteins: 7 g Fats: 4 g Carbs: 26 g

4.14 Classic Avocado Toast

Cooking Time: 5 mins, Prepping time: 5 mins, Servings: 1

Ingredients
- 1 slice hearty toasted bread
- 1 to 2 tsp. coconut oil or olive oil
- 1/4 ripe avocado, sliced
- 1/8 tsp. sea salt

Directions
1. Put avocado slices on top of the olive oil spread bread. Extra oil may be drizzled on top if desired after the avocado has been gently mashed. Sprinkle salt over the top.

Nutritional Facts:
Calories: 160 Kcal Proteins: 3 g Fats: 11 g Carbs: 15 g

4.15 Buttermilk Pumpkin Waffles

Cooking Time: 5 mins, Prepping time: 20 mins, Servings: 12 waffles

Ingredients

- 3/4 cup flour
- 1/2 cup wheat flour
- 2 tbsp. brown sugar
- 1 tsp. baking powder
- 1 tsp. ground cinnamon
- 1/2 tsp. ground ginger
- 1/4 tsp. baking soda
- 1/4 tsp. salt
- 1/4 tsp. ground cloves
- 2 large eggs
- 1 1/4 cups buttermilk
- 1/2 cup pumpkin, fresh or canned
- 2 tbsp. butter, melted
- Optional: maple syrup and butter

Directions
1. In a mixing bowl, add the first nine ingredients and mix well. Combine the pumpkin, eggs, melted butter and buttermilk in a small bowl and stir to combine. Just enough liquid should be added to the dry components to make them come together.
2. Bake until golden brown in a heated waffle machine, following the manufacturer's instructions. If you'd like, top with butter and maple syrup.
3. Alternatively, you may freeze the finished waffles. Freeze in a sealed container between sheets of waxed paper. Reheat the waffle in a microwave on the medium setting for best results. Use immediately. Alternatively, cook each waffle in the microwave for about 30-60 seconds, depending on the size.

Nutritional Facts:
Calories: 194 Kcal Proteins: 7 g Fats: 6 g Carbs: 28 g

4.16 Southwest Breakfast Wraps

Prepping time: 15 mins, Cooking Time: 15 mins, Servings: 4

Ingredients
- 1 tbsp. olive oil
- 1 onion, chopped
- 1/2 cup fresh mushrooms, sliced
- 1 green chili, chopped
- 1 red pepper, chopped
- Jalapeno pepper, chopped
- 1 can green chilies, chopped
- 1 minced garlic clove
- 8 egg whites
- 1/4 cup grated Mexican cheese
- 4 whole wheat tortillas

Direction
1. Warm the oil in a nonstick pan on medium-high heat. Cook and stir the peppers, onion, mushrooms, chilies, and garlic until crisp-tender. Keep heated after removing from pan.
2. Egg whites and cheese should be combined in a mixing bowl before using. Cook and whisk on medium heat till the egg whites start setting and no liquid egg is left. Put the egg white combination in the pan.
3. Add 1 tbsp. egg white mixture and a dollop of the vegetable mixture to each tortilla.. Roll up the tortilla, folding in the bottom and the edges over the filling as you go.

Nutritional Facts
Calories: 254 Kcal Proteins: 14 g Fats: 8 g Carbs: 29 g

4.17 Lance's French Toast

Prepping time: 20 mins, Cooking Time: 10 mins, Servings: 6

Ingredients

- 4 eggs
- 1 cup milk
- 1 tbsp. honey
- 1/2 tsp. ground cinnamon
- 1/8 tsp. pepper
- 12 slices wheat bread

Directions

1. Whisk the eggs, cinnamon, milk, pepper, and honey together in a large bowl. Bread should be dipped in a mixture of eggs on both sides. Cook for 3 to 4 mins on a hot, oiled griddle till golden brown.
2. To serve, top with cinnamon sugar or a vanilla frosting, if preferred.
3. Option to freeze: Cool on the wire racks before serving. Use a resealable freezer jar to freeze among layers of waxed paper. To defrost, reheat the French toast on medium heat in the toaster oven. Alternatively, you may cook up each piece of French toast in the microwave for 30 to 60 seconds, depending on your microwave.

Nutritional Facts:
Calories: 218 Kcal Proteins: 13 g Fats: 6 g Carbs: 28 g

4.18 Whole Wheat Pecan Waffles

Prepping time: 10 mins, Cooking Time: 20 mins, Servings: 6 waffles

Ingredients

- 2 cups pastry wheat flour
- 2 tbsp. sugar
- 3 tsp. baking powder
- 1/2 tsp. salt
- 2 eggs
- 1 3/4 cups milk
- 1/4 cup canola oil
- 1/2 cup chopped pecans

Directions

1. Set waffle maker to high heat. Mix the first four ingredients and stir until smooth in a bowl. In a separate dish, whisk all together with egg yolks, oil, and milk. Stir this into the flour mixture till barely moistened.
2. Beat the egg whites till they are stiff and not dry in a separate bowl. Add to the batter by folding in. Depending on the manufacturer's instructions, cook the waffles until golden brown, then sprinkle the batter with chopped nuts before serving.
3. Option to freeze: Freeze in the freezer between sheets of waxed paper. Defrost in the toaster or broiler on medium heat.

Nutritional Facts:
Calories: 241 Kcal Proteins: 7 g Fats: 14 g Carbs: 24 g

4.19 Portobello Mushrooms Florentine

Prepping time: 10 mins, Cooking Time: 15 mins, Servings: 2

Ingredients
- 2 large mushrooms
- Spray for cooking
- 1/8 tsp. garlic salt
- 1/8 tsp. pepper
- 1/2 tsp. olive oil
- 1 chopped onion
- 1 cup baby spinach, fresh
- 2 eggs
- 1/8 tsp. salt
- 1/4 cup goat cheese
- Fresh basil, minced

Directions
1. To begin, preheat the oven to 425°F. Place sprayed mushrooms in a 15 by 10 by 1-inch baking dish. Place the pan with the stem side down. Add pepper and salt to taste, along with some minced garlic. Bake for 10 mins, uncovered, until fork-tender.
2. Then, in a medium nonstick pan, heat oil and cook onion until soft, about 10 mins. Stir in spinach and cook until it is wilted for about 2 mins.
3. Beat together the eggs and the salt in a separate bowl before adding them to the frying pan. Prepare by cooking and stirring the eggs until they are completely thickened and the liquid has evaporated. Add cheese and basil if used.

Nutritional Facts
Calories: 126 Kcal Proteins: 11 g Fats: 5 g Carbs: 10 g

4.20 Apple Walnut Pancakes

Prepping time: 15 mins, Cooking Time: 15 mins, Servings: 18 pancakes

Ingredients

- 1 cup flour
- 1 cup wheat flour
- 1 tbsp. brown sugar
- 2 tsp. baking powder
- 1 tsp. salt
- 2 egg whites
- 1 beaten egg
- 2 cups milk, fat-free
- 2 tbsp. canola oil
- 1 apple, chopped and peeled
- 1/2 cup walnuts, chopped
- Maple syrup

Directions

1. The first step is to take a bowl and mix all of the ingredients. Mix the eggs, milk, egg whites, and oil until well combined in a separate dish. Stir only unless dry ingredients are moistened. Add the walnuts and apple and combine well.
2. Use a cooking spray-coated grill to heat. Place batter on a heated griddle in 1/4 cup portions. In other words, cook until the bubbles start to burst on top and the bottoms become golden in color. Turn the pan over and continue cooking until the second side is golden brown. Serve with maple syrup, if desired.
3. Option to freeze: Using waxed paper between layers of pancakes, store them in a freezer container that can be sealed. Reheat the pancakes for 6-10 minutes at 375 degrees Fahrenheit on a nonstick baking sheet wrapped in aluminium foil. Put 3 pancakes over the microwave plate and cook in the microwave for one and a half mins, depending on your microwave.

Nutritional Facts:
Calories: 208 Kcal Proteins: 8 g Fats: 8 g Carbs: 27 g

4.21 Mixed Fruit with Lemon-Basil Dressing

Prepping time: 5 mins, Cooking Time: 10 mins, Servings: 8

Ingredients

- 2 tbsp. lemon juice
- ½ tsp. sugar
- 1/4 tsp. salt
- ¼ tsp. ground mustard
- 1/8 tsp. onion powder
- Dash of pepper
- 6 tbsp. olive oil
- 4 1/2 tsp. minced basil
- 1 cup pineapple
- 1 cup strawberries, sliced
- 1 cup kiwifruit, sliced and peeled
- 1 cup watermelon balls, seedless
- 1 cup fresh blueberries
- 1 cup fresh raspberries

Directions

1. Put the lemon juice, salt, sugar, mustard, pepper, and onion powder in a blender or food processor and blend for seconds until smooth. Stream in the oil steadily while processing is going on. Lastly, stir in the basil until everything is well combined.
2. In a large bowl, mix the fruit well. Toss in the dressing and coat well. Keep chilled until ready to serve.

Nutritional Facts:

Calories: 145 Kcal Proteins: 1 g Fats: 11 g Carbs: 14 g

4.22 Flaxseed Oatmeal Pancakes

Prepping time: 10 mins, Cooking Time: 15 mins, Servings: 4 pancakes

Ingredients

- 1/3 cup wheat flour
- 3 tbsp. oats
- 1 tbsp. flaxseed
- ½ tsp. baking powder
- ¼ tsp. ground cinnamon
- 1/8 tsp. baking soda
- Dash of salt
- 1 egg
- ½ cup buttermilk
- 1 tbsp. brown sugar
- 1 tbsp. canola oil
- ½ tsp. vanilla extract

Direction:

1. Mix the first seven ingredients in a bowl. Set aside. In a bowl, stir the buttermilk and egg yolk together until smooth. Add the vanilla extract, brown sugar, and oil, and mix until well-combined.
2. By using a mixer at medium speed, Beat the egg whites until stiff peaks form. Add to the batter by folding in.
3. When bubbling form on the top of the batter, flip it over with a spatula. Cook the other side until it's golden and crisp.

Nutritional Facts

Calories: 273 Kcal Proteins: 10 g Fats: 13 g Carbs: 31 g

4.23 Confetti Scrambled Egg Pockets

Prepping time: 10 mins, Cooking Time: 10 mins, Servings: 6

Ingredients

- 1 cup frozen corn
- ¼ cup chopped green pepper
- 2 tbsp chopped onion
- 1 jar diced pimientos
- 1 tbsp. butter
- 8 eggs
- ¼ cup evaporated milk, reduced fat
- ½ tsp. seasoned salt
- 1 chopped tomato
- 1 onion, sliced
- 6 whole wheat pita halves
- Salsa (optional)

Directions

1. Sauté the corn, onion, green peppers, and pimientos in butter in a large nonstick pan for 5-7 mins, or until soft.
2. Put salt and pepper to taste in a big bowl and whisk together. In a medium saucepan, cook and whisk the eggs until they are fully set, about 10 mins. Add tomato and scallions to the mixture and mix to combine well.
3. Fill every pita half approximately two-thirds of the way with the soup. If desired, top with salsa.

Nutritional Facts

Calories: 224 Kcal Proteins: 13 g Fats: 9 g Carbs: 24 g

4.24 Whole Wheat Pancakes

Prepping time: 10 mins, Cooking Time: 15 mins, Servings: 20 pancakes

Ingredients

- 2 cups wheat flour
- ½ cup toasted wheat germ
- 1 tsp. baking soda
- ½ tsp. salt
- 2 eggs
- 3 cups buttermilk
- 1 tbsp. canola oil

Directions

1. Salt and baking soda should be combined in a small bowl with the flour. Whisk the eggs, buttermilk, and oil together in a separate dish. Just enough dry components should be stirred into wet ingredients to mix.
2. When bubbles begin to develop on the surface of the batter, use a spatula to flip it over. Cook the second side until it's golden and crisp.
3. Option to freeze: Place cooled pancakes in a sealed freezer jar between sheets of waxed paper. On a nonstick baking sheet, place the pancakes, wrap them with aluminum foil, and reheat for 6-10 mins in a heated 375°F oven. Alternatively, stack three pancakes high on the plate and cook on high for 45-90 seconds, depending on the thickness of the pancakes.

Nutritional Facts:
Calories: 157 Kcal Proteins: 09 g Fats: 4 g Carbs: 24 g

4.25 Chicken Brunch Bake

Prepping time: 15 mins, Cooking Time: 60 mins, Servings: 8

Ingredients

- 9 slices of day-old bread, cubed
- 3 cups chicken broth
- 4 cups cubed cooked chicken
- ½ cup uncooked instant rice

- ½ cup diced pimientos
- 2 tbsp. minced fresh parsley
- ½ tsp. salt (optional)
- 4 eggs, beaten

Directions

1. Mix bread pieces and broth in a large basin. Rice, parsley, pimientos, and salt may all be added at this point, but it's not necessary. Place the mixture in a greased 13 by 9-inch baking dish. Over everything, pour the beaten eggs.
2. Serve warm or at room temperature.
3. Bake at 325°F for 60 mins, uncovering halfway through baking.

Nutritional Facts
Calories: 233 Kcal Proteins: 18 g Fats: 6 g Carbs: 18 g

4.26 Shakshuka

Prepping time: 10 mins, Cooking Time: 25 mins, Servings: 4

Ingredients

- 2 tbsp. olive oil
- 1 finely chopped onion,
- 1 clove garlic, chopped
- 1 tsp. ground cumin
- Kosher salt and pepper
- 1 lb. tomatoes
- 8 eggs
- ¼ cup chopped baby spinach
- For serving, toasted baguette

Directions

1. Preheat the oven to 400°F. Oil should be heated in a big oven-safe pan at a medium-high temperature. Add the onion and cook for 8 mins, or until it is lightly browned and soft.
2. Cook for one min after adding the cumin, garlic, and a half-teaspoon of pepper and salt. Add the tomatoes and roast for 10 mins in the oven, stirring occasionally.
3. Remove the pan from the oven, stir the vegetable mixture, and create with these 8 little wells, then gently break one egg into each one. Bake the eggs for 7 to 8 mins for somewhat runny yolks, depending on how you want them. Optionally, serve with bread and top with fresh spinach before digging in.

Nutritional Facts
Calories: 235 Kcal Proteins: 14 g Fats: 16 g Carbs: 8 g

4.27 Chilled Overnight Chia

Prepping time: 10 mins, Cooking Time: 15 mins, Servings: 4

Ingredients

Milk & Honey

- 2 cups old-fashioned oats
- 4 tbsp. chia seeds
- 4 tbsp. honey
- Milk

Blueberry-Coconut

- 2 cups of old-fashioned oats
- 4 tbsp. chia seeds
- 4 tbsp. honey
- 3 cups coconut milk
- 1 tsp. lemon zest
- Fresh blueberries

Brownie Batter

- 2 cups old-fashioned oats
- 4 tbsp. chia seeds
- 4 tbsp. honey
- Milk
- 4 tbsp. cocoa powder, unsweetened
- 4 tbsp. chocolate-hazelnut spread
- Toasted hazelnuts, chopped

PB&J

- 2 cups old-fashioned oats
- 4 tbsp. chia seeds
- 4 tbsp. honey
- Milk
- 4 tbsp. peanut butter
- 4 tbsp. strawberry jam
- Sliced strawberries

Directions

Milk & Honey

1. Add 1 tbsp. of chia seeds, 1/2 cup oats, 2/3 cup milk, and 1 tbsp. honey to 4 16-oz. containers. Shake well to ensure everything is well combined. Then refrigerate.

Blueberry-Coconut

2. Add 1 tbsp. of chia seeds, 1/2 cup of oats, 3/4 cup coconut milk, and 1 tbsp. of honey to every 4 16-oz. containers. Refrigerate after covering and shaking to mix. To serve, add blueberries and 1/4 tsp. of lemon zest to each container.

Brownie Batter

3. Mix 1 tbsp. of chia seeds, 1/2 cup of oats, 1 tbsp. of honey, 1 tbsp. cocoa powder and 2/3 cup milk to 4 16-oz. jars and mix well. Refrigerate after covering and shaking to mix. Then, add 1 tbsp. chocolate-hazelnut spread and hazelnuts to each jar once the chocolate has soaked up and let cool.

PB&J

4. Stir in 1 tbsp. of honey and 2/3 cup of milk to each of the 4 16-oz cups, plus 1/2 cup of oats. Refrigerate after covering and shaking to mix. Add one spoonful of peanut butter to each jar once it's been soaked, followed by one tbsp. of strawberry jam with fresh strawberries to decorate each one.

Nutritional Facts
Calories: 157 Kcal Proteins: 09 g Fats: 4 g Carbs: 24 g

4.28 Classic Omelet and Greens

Prepping time: 5 mins, Cooking Time: 15 mins, Servings: 4

Ingredients

- 3 tbsp. olive oil
- 1 onion, chopped
- 8 eggs
- Kosher salt
- 2 tbsp. unsalted butter
- 1 oz. grated parmesan
- 2 tbsp. lemon juice
- 3 oz. spinach

Directions

1. Heat 1 tbsp. oil in a pan over medium-high heat. Put the onion and cook for approximately 5 mins, or until it is soft. Put the mixture in a small basin and set aside.
2. Whisk 1 tbsp. water, eggs, and 1 tsp. salt in a separate bowl until smooth. Turn to medium-high heat and add the butter to the skillet. Toss in the eggs and heat them until they are just starting to set, continuously swirling with a spoon. Cook eggs until just set, 3-4 mins, over low heat with the lid on the pan. Fold in half and sprinkle parmesan and sautéed onion, if using.
3. Lemon juice and the 2 tbsp. olive oil should be combined in a separate bowl. Serve the omelet with the spinach and vinaigrette you made earlier.

Nutritional Facts
Calories: 330 Kcal Proteins: 16 g Fats: 27 g Carbs: 6 g

4.29 Berry Yogurt Bowl

Prepping time: 5 mins, Cooking Time: 5 mins, Servings: 1

Ingredients

- ¾ cup yogurt
- 1 tbsp. chopped mint
- 2 ½ tbsp. chopped walnuts
- ½ cup min and citrus berries

Directions

1. In a bowl, combine the yoghurt and stir thoroughly with a spoon. Min berries and citrus, walnuts and min make a delicious garnish.
2. Keep refrigerated/consumed fresh.

Nutritional Facts:
Calories: 70 Kcal Proteins: 4 g Fats: 20 g Carbs: 6 g

4.30 Best-Ever Granola

Prepping time: 30 mins, Cooking Time: 45 mins, Servings: 7 cups

Ingredients

- ½ cup olive oil, melted
- ¾ cup maple syrup
- 2 tbsp. turbinado sugar
- 1 tsp. Kosher salt
- 3 cups rolled oats
- 1 cup coconut flakes, unsweetened
- 3/4 cup sunflower seeds, raw
- 3/4 cup pumpkin seeds, raw

Directions

Best-Ever Granola

1. Preheat the oven to 300°F. Cover the baking pan with parchment paper and put it in the oven to bake. Combine maple syrup, oil, salt, and sugar in a large basin. Pour the oats into a well in the center and mix them together.
2. Spread the mixture onto the heated baking sheet and bake for 45-55 minutes, stirring every fifteen minutes. Allow cooling fully.

For Ginger-Pecan Granola

1. Leave out the pumpkin seeds and use only half a cup of sunflower seeds. Add 1½ cups of chopped pecans. Bake the granola according to the directions on the package, and after removing it from the oven, stir in 1 ½ tablespoon finely chopped ginger.

For Cumin-Thyme Granola

1. Leave out the coconut. Add maple syrup and oil to a bowl, along with 2 tbsp. each of cumin seeds & finely chopped thyme leaves, as well as 1 tsp. of cinnamon.

For Spicy Sesame-Tamari Granola

1. Leave sugar, sunflower seeds, and salt. Add 1 cup of pumpkin seeds to ½ cup of coconut. The oil and half-cup of tamari are combined with the half-cup of sesame seeds and the heaping half-teaspoon of cayenne pepper.

For Sweet and Spicy Granola

1. Coconut, sugar, and pumpkin seeds should be avoided. Along with the oats, add ¼ cup gently crushed coriander seeds plus 1 1/2 cups chopped almonds.

Nutritional Facts

Calories: 256 Kcal Proteins: 16 g Fats: 20 g Carbs: 6 g

4.31 Sheet Pan Sausage and Egg Breakfast Bake

Prepping time: 15 mins, Cooking Time: 35 mins, Servings: 4

Ingredients

- 4 breakfast sausages, 6 oz total
- 4 slices bacon
- 8 oz. cremini mushrooms
- 16 cocktail tomatoes, sliced
- 2 chopped cloves garlic
- 1 tbsp. olive oil
- Kosher salt and pepper
- 4 eggs
- 1/2 cup parsley
- Toast

Directions

1. Preheat the oven to 400°F. Roast the sausages and bacon for fifteen mins on the wide baking sheet and bake.
2. Toss mushrooms, garlic and tomatoes in a large mixing bowl with the oil, pepper, and salt to taste. Roast for 10 mins on a baking pan.
3. Bake until the meat is done and egg whites become translucent, 5-10 mins more. Make wells in veggies and break an egg into each one.
4. Serve with bread, if preferred, and garnish with parsley if using.

Nutritional Facts

Calories: 300 Kcal Proteins: 17 g Fats: 21 g Carbs: 10 g

4.32 Tofu Scramble

Prepping time: 5 mins, Cooking Time: 10 mins, Servings: 4

Ingredients

- ⅓ cup almond milk
- 2 tbsp. nutritional yeast
- 2 minced garlic cloves
- ½ tsp. Dijon mustard
- ¼ tsp. ground turmeric
- ¼ tsp. ground cumin
- 1 tbsp. olive oil
- ½ cup onion
- 14 oz. tofu, dry and crumbled
- Black pepper and sea salt

Directions

1. Stir nutritional yeast, almond milk, turmeric, cumin, mustard, garlic and 1/2 tsp of salt together in a small dish. Place on the back burner.
2. In a pan, heat olive oil on medium-high heat. Stir inside the onion and pinches of the salt and pepper; simmer for 5 mins. Cook about 3 to 4 mins, often stirring, until tofu gets cooked through. Mix almond milk, then turn the heat down to a simmer and remove from the heat. Stirring periodically, cook for a further 3 mins. Add black pepper to taste and salt (can add an extra ¼ to ½ tsp. at this point). If preferred, top with more vegetables, salsa, and tortillas.

Nutritional Facts
Calories: 237 Kcal Proteins: 14 g Fats: 16 g Carbs: 7 g

4.33 Pumpkin Protein Pancakes

Prepping time: 10 mins, Cooking Time: 10 mins, Servings: 3 pancakes

Ingredients

- 1 1/2 cups rolled oats
- 2/3 cup pumpkin puree
- 1/2 cup full-fat cottage cheese
- 2 eggs
- 2 tbsp. maple syrup
- 2 tsp. baking powder
- 1 tsp. pumpkin pie spice or apple pie spice
- 1/4 tsp. salt
- Suggested toppings: maple syrup, maple butter, chocolate chips, walnuts, nut butter.

Directions

1. Combine all the ingredient in a blender; mix until almost smooth (must not over blend). While the pan is getting hot, let the batter rest in the blender. Apply butter or oil to the pan to prevent sticking.
2. When the frying pan is heated, add a third of the batter to make three pancakes. To make a spherical pancake, smooth batter using the back of a wooden spoon. The pancakes should be cooked for 2–4

mins, or until they are somewhat puffy and form little bubbles on the edges. Allow it to cook for 1-2 mins on the other side before gently flipping. Turn down the heat to moderate flame if the pancakes are browning too fast.
3. To Store: Refrigerate remaining pancakes for up to 4 days in a sealed jar.
4. To reheat: Microwave pancakes on low for 30 seconds at a time until hot.
5. Let the pancakes cool completely before freezing. Once the pancakes have cooled, layer them with wax paper between each one. Freeze them up to 3 months in the zip-top bag that has been pre-heated to prevent sticking. When you're ready to dine, just reheat the frozen pancakes according to the package directions.

Nutritional Facts:
Calories: 295 Kcal Proteins: 16 g Fats: 7 g Carbs: 41 g

4.34 Avocado Toast Recipe (with Pickled Onions) (Vegan + Best Tips)

Prepping time: 5 mins, Cooking Time: 5 mins, Servings: 2

Ingredients

- 2 slices bread
- ½ small avocado
- ⅛ tsp. sea salt
- 1/8 tsp. black pepper
- Juice of ½ lime
- Pickled onions, a few slices
- Flakes of red pepper

Directions

1. Roast the bread until it becomes golden brown, about three mins on each side.
2. Then, remove avocado from its peel and put it in the bowl while the bread is browning. Mix the lime juice, sea salt and black pepper. Mash it with a fork unless it's the consistency you want.
3. On each of the toasts, equally spread the avocado.
4. Sprinkle/apply the remaining subjects, then sit back and enjoy.

Nutritional Facts:
Calories: 185 Kcal Proteins: 5 g Fats: 8 g Carbs: 25 g

4.35 Sweet Potato Kale Frittata

Prepping time: 20 mins, Cooking Time: 10 mins, Servings: 4

Ingredients

- 6 eggs
- 1 cup half-and-half
- 1 tsp. Kosher salt
- 1/2 tsp. ground pepper
- 2 sweet potatoes
- 2 tbsp. olive oil
- 2 cups sealed chopped kale
- ½ onion
- 2 cloves garlic
- 3 oz. goat cheese

Directions

1. Preheat the oven to 350°F. Combine eggs and the next three ingredients in a bowl and whisk until well combined.
2. In a 10-inch nonstick pan (ovenproof), cook sweet potatoes with 1 tbsp. of heated oil until just soft and golden, 8-10 mins; take off the heat and keep it warm. Stir in potatoes after sautéing kale and remaining two ingredients in the 1 tbsp oil for 3-4 mins or until kale has wilted and just become soft. Cook the veggies for a further 3 mins after pouring the egg mix on them. Goat cheese may be sprinkled over the beaten eggs before they are finished.
3. Bake for 10–14 mins, or when the cheese has set around 350°F.

Nutritional Facts:
Calories: 325 Kcal Proteins: 4 g Fats: 6 g Carbs: 25 g

4.36 Gruyere, Bacon, and Spinach Scrambled Eggs

Prepping time: 5 mins, Cooking Time: 10 mins, Servings: 4

Ingredients

- 8 eggs
- 1 tsp. Dijon mustard
- Pepper and Kosher salt
- 1 tbsp. olive oil
- 2 slices thick bacon, cooked
- 2 cups spinach, torn
- 2 oz. Gruyere cheese, shredded

Directions

1. In a large mixing bowl, combine Dijon mustard, eggs, 1 tbsp. water, and 1/2 tsp. pepper and salt. Whisk until combined.
2. Heat butter and oil over medium flame in non stick pan. Add the eggs and simmer for 2-3 mins for soft-medium eggs, stirring with a rubber spatula once every min. Toss in the spinach, bacon, and Gruyere cheeses until everything is well-combined.

Nutritional Facts:
Calories: 265 Kcal Proteins: 22 g Fats: 7 g Carbs: 6 g

4.37 Easy Sausage & Pepper Skillet (Paleo, Whole30, Gluten-Free)

Prepping time: 10 mins, Cooking Time: 10 mins, Servings: 2

Ingredients

- 1/2 tbsp. coconut oil
- 2 links apple sausage chicken
- 1/2 cup red peppers, sliced
- 1/2 cup yellow peppers, sliced
- 1/2 cup red onion, sliced
- 1/4 tsp. crushed red pepper flakes
- 1 clove garlic, minced
- Salt and pepper
- 1 tbsp. parsley fresh

Direction

1. Start by heating a pan to a moderate flame. Add oil to the pan after it's heated through.
2. Add your sausage and cook it from both sides; keep often stirring until it is cooked through. Add onions & peppers to the sausage after it's cooked and keep stirring. Add the garlic powder, crushed flakes of red pepper, and salt to taste.
3. The peppers should be soft and have a little sharpness, so sauté them for another 5 mins until they become opaque. Serve immediately, garnished with chopped parsley!

Nutritional Facts:
Calories: 179 Kcal Proteins: 5.5 g Fats: 13 g Carbs: 10 g

4.38 Fruity Yogurt Parfait

Prepping time: 5 mins, Cooking Time: 0 mins, Servings: 1

Ingredients

- 1 cup mixed berries, frozen
- 1 cup Greek yogurt
- 1 tbsp. flaxseed
- 1 tsp. vanilla extract
- 1/2 kiwi
- ¼ cup blueberries
- 3 tbsp nut clusters and grains fruit

Directions

1. Frozen berries, yogurt, vanilla extract and flaxseed should be blended until smooth in a food processor.
2. Top with blueberries, kiwi and fruit and nut clusters once you've transferred the yogurt mixture to the bowl.

Nutritional Facts:
Calories: 300 Kcal Proteins: 7 g Fats: 5 g Carbs: 16 g

Chapter 5 Lunch Recipes

5.1 Curried Chicken Skillet

Prepping time: 10 mins, Cooking Time: 20 mins, Servings: 4

Ingredients

- 1 1/3 cups + 1/2 cup reduced sodium chicken broth, divided
- 2/3 cup rinsed quinoa
- 1 tbsp. canola oil
- 1 diced sweet potato
- 1 chopped onion
- 1 chopped celery rib
- 1 cup frozen peas
- 2 cloves minced garlic
- 1 tsp. minced gingerroot
- 3 tsp. curry powder
- ¼ tsp. salt
- 2 cups chicken, shredded and cooked

Directions

1. To begin, heat 1 1/3 cups of broth over medium-high heat, stirring constantly. Quinoa may be added to the dish. Low the heat to a simmer and cover the pan for 12-15 mins, or until the liquid has been absorbed.

2. Heat the oil medium saucepan. Fry onion, sweet potato, and celery for 10-12 mins, unless potato is cooked. Continue cooking for 2 mins with peas, ginger, garlic, and spices. Add the chicken as well as the rest of the stock and cook through on the stovetop. Add in the quinoa and mix well to combine the flavors.

Nutritional Facts:
Calories: 367 Kcal Proteins: 29 g Fats: 11 g Carbs: 39 g

5.2 Pressure-Cooker Pork Tacos with Mango Salsa

Prepping time: 25 mins, Cooking Time: 5 mins, Servings: 12

Ingredients

- 2 tbsp. white vinegar
- 2 tbsp. lime juice
- 3 cups pineapple, cubed fresh
- 1 red onion, chopped
- 3 tbsp. chili powder
- 2 chipotle peppers
- 2 tsp. ground cumin
- 1 1/2 tsp. salt
- 1/2 tsp. pepper
- 1 bottle of Mexican beer, dark
- 3 pounds pork tenderloin, 1-inch cubes
- 1/4 cup fresh cilantro, chopped
- 1 jar mango salsa
- 24 corn tortillas, warmed
- Optional toppings: cubed avocado, cubed fresh pineapple, queso fresco

Directions

1. Blend the very first nine components until smooth, then add beer and mix well. Pineapple & pork should be combined in a 6-quart pressure cooker. Close the cooker after locking the lid. Set the timer for 3 mins on high flame in the pressure cooker. Use pressure that releases quickly. At the very least, the internal temperature of pork should be 145°F. Break up the meat with a spoon.
2. Add cilantro to the salsa and mix well. Serve pork mix in tacos with a slotted spoon, adding salsa and other toppings to taste.
3. Frozen suggestion: Freeze the cooked meat combination and any cooking liquids that remain in the pot after cooling. To use, let stand in the fridge overnight to defrost slightly. Stirring periodically, bring to a boil in a large pot.

Nutritional Facts:
Calories: 284 Kcal Proteins: 26 g Fats: 6 g Carbs: 30 g

5.3 Chicken with Peach-Avocado Salsa

Prepping time: 10 mins, Cooking Time: 20 mins, Servings: 4

Ingredients

- 1 peeled peach, chopped
- 1 ripe peeled avocado, cubed
- ½ cup red pepper, chopped
- 3 tbsp. red onion, finely chopped
- 1 tbsp. basil, minced
- 1 tbsp. lime juice
- 1 tsp. pepper sauce
- ½ tsp. grated lime zest
- 3/4 tsp. salt, divided
- 1/2 tsp. pepper, divided
- 4 chicken breast halves, boneless & skinless

Directions

1. Salsa: In a mixing bowl, mix avocado, red pepper, peaches, onion, lime juice, basil, lime zest, hot sauce, 1/4 tsp pepper and 1/4 teaspoon of salt
2. Add the last of the pepper and salt to the chicken before serving. Grill the chicken for 5 mins, covered, on a lightly oiled grill rack set to medium heat. Grill for a further 7-9 mins, or until an instant-read thermometer registers 165°F. Serve with something like a salsa if desired.

Nutritional Facts:
Calories: 367 Kcal Proteins: 29 g Fats: 11 g Carbs: 39 g

5.4 Pressure-Cooker Italian Shrimp 'n' Pasta

Prepping time: 20 mins, Cooking Time: 20 mins, Servings: 6

Ingredients

- 2 tbsp. canola oil
- 1lb. chicken thighs, boneless and skinless
- 1 can crushed tomatoes
- 1 1/2 cups water
- 2 chopped celery ribs
- 1 green pepper, 1-inch pieces
- 1 chopped onion
- 2 minced garlic cloves
- 1 tbsp. sugar
- 1/2 tsp. salt
- 1/2 tsp. Italian seasoning
- 1/8 - 1/4 tsp. cayenne pepper
- 1 bay leaf
- 1 cup uncooked orzo (pasta)
- 1 lb. cooked shrimp, peeled and deveined

Directions

1. Choose medium heat on a 6-quart pressure cooker's sauté setting. Add 1 tbsp. of oil to the mixture. Cook the chicken in the batches in heated oil, adding more oil as necessary. Use the 'cancel' button; add the remaining 11 ingredients and mix well. Close the pressure cooker after locking the lid. Set the timer for 8 mins on medium flame in the pressure cooker. Use a pressure that releases quickly. To end the program, use the 'cancel' button
2. Put the bay leaf out and throw it away. Choose the sauté option and set the temperature to medium. Add the orzo and mix well to combine the flavors again. Stir frequently till the pasta is cooked through

to the desired doneness. Put the shrimp and cook for a further 2 mins, stirring occasionally. Select the cancel button.

Nutritional Facts
Calories: 418 Kcal Proteins: 36 g Fats: 12 g Carbs: 40 g

5.5 Tuna Teriyaki Kabobs

Prepping time: 25 mins, Cooking Time: 15 mins, Servings: 8

Ingredients

- 1 1/2 lb. tuna steaks
- 2 red peppers, sweet
- 1 onion chopped into 1-inch pieces

Marinade/dressing

- 1/4 cup minced cilantro
- 1/4 cup sesame oil
- 3 tbsp. lime juice
- 2 tbsp. soy sauce
- 2 tbsp. olive oil
- 1 tbsp. minced gingerroot
- 2 minced garlic cloves

Salad

- 1 package of baby spinach
- 1 yellow pepper, medium and sweet
- 8 tomatoes

Directions

1. Thread the tuna pieces on 4 metal or wet wooden skewers. Four additional skewers will be needed to hold the peppers and onions. Put the skewers on a baking sheet and bake for about 20 mins.
2. Stir all marinade ingredients in a bowl and whisk to combine. Half of the mix may be used to make salad dressing. Put it in the fridge, covered, for 30 mins with leftover marinade poured on skewers.
3. Cover and grill the kabobs over moderate heat on greased grill rack, turning them periodically, until the tuna becomes slightly pink throughout the middle (about 2 mins on each side) and the veggies are crisp-tender (about 10-12 mins). Immediately remove and reserve the warm tuna kabobs while finishing cooking veggies.
4. Keep 1 tbsp of dressing for salad and then use it over the spinach, cherry tomatoes and yellow pepper. Serve a tuna kabob as well as a veggie kabob with a salad on each plate.

Nutritional Facts:
Calories: 389 Kcal Proteins: 45 g Fats: 11 g Carbs: 15 g

5.6 Chicken & Spanish Cauliflower "Rice"

Prepping time: 30 mins, Cooking Time: 20 mins, Servings: 4

Ingredients

- 1 cauliflower
- 1lb. chicken breasts, boneless and skinless, ½-inch cubes
- 1/2 tsp. salt
- 1/2 tsp. pepper
- 1 tbsp. canola oil
- 1 chopped green pepper
- 1 chopped onion
- 1 minced garlic clove
- 1/2 cup tomato juice
- 1/4 tsp. ground cumin
- 1/4 cup chopped cilantro
- 1 tbsp. lime juice

Directions

1. Cauliflower should be cored and sliced into 1-inch pieces. Process the cauliflower until it looks like rice by pulsing it in small batches in a food processor.
2. Season the chicken using pepper and salt and put it in the dish. Heat the oil in the pan over medium-high heat; cook chicken for 5 mins or until barely browned. Continue cooking for 3 mins after adding the onion, green pepper, and garlic.
3. Bring to a simmer, stirring in the cumin and tomato juice at this point. Cook the cauliflower for 7-10 mins, stirring periodically, covered, over a moderate flame. Then add lime juice and fresh coriander and mix well.

Nutritional Facts:
Calories: 227 Kcal Proteins: 28 g Fats: 7 g Carbs: 15 g

5.7 Grilled Chicken Chopped Salad

Prepping time: 30 mins, Cooking Time: 20 mins, Servings: 4

Ingredients

- 1lb. chicken tenderloins
- 6 tbsp. salad dressing, zesty Italian, divided
- 2 zucchini, quartered lengthwise
- 1 quartered red onion
- 2 ears sweet corn, husks removed
- 1 bunch romaine, chopped
- 1 chopped cucumber
- Additional salad dressing

Directions

1. Put the chicken to a large bowl and add 4 tbsp. of the dressing; stir to coat. Use the leftover 2 tbsp. of dressing to brush on onion and zucchini.
2. Close the cover and grill the corn, onion and zucchini over medium flame. Frill the onion and zucchini for 2-3 mins on each side or till soft. Grill the corn for 10-12 mins, flipping it over halfway through cooking time.

3. Pat chicken dry with paper towels after removing it from the marinade. Grill the chicken for 3-4 mins, covered, over medium heat, until it is no longer pink.
4. Chop vegetables into small pieces. Remove corn kernels from cobs. Layer grilled veggies, romaine, chicken and cucumber in a custard dish or glass bowl. Serve with even more dressing, if preferred.

Nutritional Facts
Calories: 239 Kcal Proteins: 32 g Fats: 5 g Carbs: 21 g

5.8 Fish Tacos with Berry Salsa

Prepping time: 30 mins, Cooking Time: 20 mins, Servings: 4

Ingredients

- 1 cup peeled jicama, chopped
- 1 cup chopped strawberries
- 1 jalapeno pepper, finely chopped and deseeded
- 3 tbsp. minced cilantro
- 2 tbsp. lime juice
- 1/2 tsp. salt, divided
- 4 fillets tilapia
- ¼ tsp. pepper
- 8 corn tortillas
- 1/2 cup Cotija cheese, crumbled

Directions

1. Prepare the oven for broiling by preheating it at a high temperature. To make salsa, mix the first 5 ingredients in the dish and season with 1/4 tsp. salt.
2. Prepare a 15 by 10 by 1-inch baking tray by lining it using aluminum foil and placing the fillets inside it. After 5-7 minutes of broiling at a distance of 4-6 inches from the flame, the fish should be flaky when checked with a fork. Assemble fish tacos with salsa and shredded cheese, then serve.

Nutritional Facts:
Calories: 329 Kcal Proteins: 38 g Fats: 8 g Carbs: 29 g

5.9 Chicken with Fire-Roasted Tomatoes

Prepping time: 30 mins, Cooking Time: 20 mins, Servings: 4

Ingredients

- 2 tbsp. garlic herb, salt-free
- 1/2 tsp. salt
- 1/4 tsp. Italian seasoning
- 1/4 tsp. pepper
- 1/8 tsp. crushed red pepper flakes
- 4 chicken breast halves, boneless and skinless
- 1 tbsp. olive oil
- 1 can dice fire-roasted tomatoes, undrained
- ¾ lb. green beans, trimmed

- 2 tbsp. water
- 1 tbsp. butter
- Pasta, cooked

Directions

1. Combine the seasoning ingredients and apply to the chicken breasts on each side. Over medium flame warms the oil in a big pan. Sprinkle each side of the chicken with a little oil and cook until done. Bring the mixture to a boil, then add the tomatoes. Cook for 10-12 mins, covered, until a thermometer put into the thickest part of the chicken registers 165°F.
2. Then, mix green beans and water in a 2-quart microwave dish; microwave on high heat, covered, about 3-4 mins or till tender. Then drain.
3. Store heated chicken that has been removed from the skillet. The tomato mix should be thickened with the help of butter and beans. Serve with grilled chicken plus pasta if you'd like.

Nutritional Facts
Calories: 294 Kcal Proteins: 37 g Fats: 10 g Carbs: 15 g

5.10 Grilled Pork Noodle Salad

Prepping time: 40 mins, Cooking Time: 5 mins, Servings: 6

Ingredients
- 1 minced jalapeno pepper
- 3 tbsp. lime juice
- 2 tbsp. fish sauce
- 2 tsp. brown sugar
- 2 pork tenderloins (3/4 pound each), cut into 1/2-inch slices
- 1 package vermicelli-style thin rice noodles

Dressing
- 1/4 cup water
- 2 tbsp. lime juice
- 1 tbsp. fish sauce
- 1/2 tsp. brown sugar

Salad
- 2 cups shredded lettuce
- 2 sliced plum tomatoes
- 1 cucumber
- 2 carrots
- 1/2 cup chopped cilantro
- 1/4 cup fresh mint, loosely packed leaves

Directions

1. Serve with rice or noodles, then top with fish sauce and brown sugar. Make a well-coated addition of pork and flip it to coat completely. Make the night before and refrigerate, covered, for at least three hours.
2. Remove meat from marinade and discard. Grill the pork, covered, for 1-2 mins till it reaches a temperature of 145°F on a grilling rack carefully sprayed with cooking spray.

3. Drain, then rinse with cold water, then squeeze out all the water completely. Dressing ingredients should be whisked together in a small bowl. Six bowls of rice noodles should be served. Toss together the noodles, veggies, pork, and herbs in the dressing.

Nutritional Facts
Calories: 315 Kcal Proteins: 27 g Fats: 4 g Carbs: 40 g

5.11 Naked Fish Tacos

Prepping time: 25 mins, Cooking Time: 10 mins, Servings:

Ingredients

- 1 cup coleslaw mix
- 1/4 cup chopped fresh cilantro
- 1 onion, sliced
- 1 tsp. jalapeno pepper, chopped
- 4 tsp. canola oil, divided
- 2 tsp. lime juice
- 1/2 tsp. ground cumin
- 1/2 tsp. salt, divided
- 1/4 tsp. pepper, divided
- 2 fillets tilapia
- 1/2 ripe avocado, sliced and peeled

Directions

1. Start with 4 items in a bowl, then add 2 tbsp. of oil, 1/8 tsp. pepper, lime juice, cumin and 1/4 tsp. of salt to the mixture and stir well. Keep chilled until ready to serve.
2. Using paper towels, pat the fillets dry and season with the leftover pepper and salt to taste. Cook tilapia till it flakes readily using a fork, 3-4 mins each side, in the leftover oil in the pan over medium-high heat. Add avocado and slaw on the top to complete the dish.

Nutritional Facts:
Calories: 293 Kcal Proteins: 33 g Fats: 16 g Carbs: 6 g

5.12 Simple Sesame Chicken with Couscous

Prepping time: 25 mins, Cooking Time: 15 mins, Servings: 4

Ingredients

- 1 1/2 cups water
- 1 cup wheat couscous
- 1 tbsp. olive oil
- 2 cups coleslaw mix
- 4 onions, sliced
- 2 tbsp + 1/2 cup of salad dressing, toasted
- 2 cups chicken breast, shredded and cooked
- 2 tbsp. minced cilantro
- Chopped peanuts

Directions

1. Boil the water at the beginning. Add the couscous and mix well. Leave covered for 5-10 mins till the water has evaporated after removing from heat. Fork-fluff the potatoes.
2. Heat oil over medium flame in a nonstick frying pan. Cook and whisk the coleslaw mix for 3-4 mins, till it is barely soft. Bring all the mix to a boil and then reduce heat to low. Stir in green onions and the remaining 2 tbsp. of dressing, then cook through. Keep couscous warm by removing it from the pan.
3. Cook and stir the remaining chicken and dressing in the same skillet over medium flame until well cooked. Top with peanuts and cilantro if preferred and served with couscous.

Nutritional Facts:
Calories: 320 Kcal Proteins: 26 g Fats: 9 g Carbs: 35 g

5.13 Mediterranean Grilled Chicken & Greens

Prepping time: 15 mins, Cooking Time: 10 mins, Servings: 4

Ingredients

- 1/4 cup orange juice
- 6 minced garlic cloves
- 1 tbsp. balsamic vinegar
- 1 1/2 tsp. dried thyme
- 1/2 tsp. salt
- 4 chicken breasts, boneless and skinless
- 2 packages mixed salad greens
- 2 cups cherry tomatoes,
- 1/2 cup feta cheese, crumbled
- 1/4 cup Greek olives, pitted and halved
- 1/4 cup prepared vinaigrette

Directions

1. Mix the first 5 ingredients in a resealable plastic bag. Then add the chicken and close the bag. Turn the coat well. Refrigerate for at least 8 hours, preferably up to 24 hours before serving.
2. Remove chicken from marinade and discard. To gently coat the grill rack, wet a towel using cooking oil and massage it over with lengthy tongs. Cook the chicken for 5-6 mins on both sides or until it reaches a temperature of 165°F by grilling it covered over medium flame or broiling it 4 inches from the flame.
3. Then mix the greens with the feta cheese and tomatoes in a big bowl and add the olives on top. Toss with vinaigrette to combine flavors. Serve the chicken sliced thinly with a side salad.

Nutritional Fact:
Calories: 282 Kcal Proteins: 33 g Fats: 11 g Carbs: 12 g

5.14 Sesame Turkey Stir-Fry

Prepping time: 20 mins, Cooking Time: 10 mins, Servings:

Ingredients

- 1 tsp. cornstarch
- 1/2 cup water
- 2 tbsp. soy sauce
- 1 tbsp. honey
- 2 tsp. curry powder
- 1/8 tsp. red pepper, crushed
- 2 tsp. canola oil
- 1 red pepper
- 1 onion, thin wedges
- 1 minced garlic clove
- 2 cups turkey breast, shredded and cooked
- 1 onion, sliced
- 2 cups brown rice, cooked
- Thin slices of serrano pepper and sesame seeds, toasted

Direction

1. Stir the first six ingredients. Heat the oil in the pan on medium heat,. Stir in the onion & red pepper and cook until they are crisp-tender, about 3 mins. Cook for a further min after adding the garlic.
2. Add cornstarch mixture to pan, stirring to combine. To thicken, cook for 2 mins, stirring constantly. Bring to a boil. Cook the turkey and thoroughly heat, adding more salt and pepper as necessary. Add the green onion and mix well. Serve over rice if desired. Add a few dashes of sriracha & sesame seeds, as preferred.

Nutritional Facts
Calories: 269 Kcal Proteins: 25 g Fats: 4 g Carbs: 32 g

5.15 Fish Tacos with Guacamole

Prepping time: 25 mins, Cooking Time: 10 mins, Servings: 4

Ingredients

- 2 cups coleslaw mix
- 1 1/2 tsp. canola oil
- 1 1/2 tsp. lime juice

Guacamole

- 1 avocado, quartered and peeled
- 2 tbsp. sour cream, fat-free
- 1 tbsp. onion, finely chopped
- 1 tbsp. minced cilantro
- 1/8 tsp. salt
- Dash of pepper

Tacos

- 1lb. tilapia fillets, 1-inch pieces
- 1/4 tsp. salt
- 1/8 tsp. pepper
- 2 tsp. canola oil
- 8 corn tortillas, warmed
- Optional toppings: chopped tomatoes, hot pepper sauce, jalapeno pepper and green onions

Directions

1. Pour coleslaw mix with lime juice and oil in a medium basin; chill until ready to serve. Mash avocado using a fork and combine it with cilantro, onion, salt and sour cream, and pepper in a separate bowl.
2. Toss pepper and salt into the tilapia, then serve. Heat the oil on medium-high flame until shimmering in a nonstick frying pan. Add tilapia and cook for 3-4 mins on both sides, or unless it starts to flake readily when tested with a fork. Top with guacamole, slaw, and any preferred ingredients, then serve with tortillas.

Nutritional Facts:
Calories: 308 Kcal Proteins: 25 g Fats: 12 g Carbs: 28 g

5.16 Grilled Steak Salad with Tomatoes & Avocado

Prepping time: 30 mins, Cooking Time: 10 mins, Servings: 6

Ingredients

- 1 sirloin steak
- 1 tbsp. olive oil
- 3 tsp. Creole seasoning
- 2 chopped tomatoes
- 1 can cannellini beans, drained and rinsed
- 1 can black beans, drained and rinsed
- 3 green onions, chopped
- 1/4 cup minced cilantro
- 2 tsp. lemon zest, grated
- 2 tbsp. lemon juice
- 1/4 tsp. salt
- 1 avocado, cubed and peeled

Directions

1. Spread Creole seasoning on both sides of the steak and coat with oil. Grill the chicken on a medium flame for 5 to 8 mins on both sides till the chicken become golden brown. Then allow it to rest for 5 mins.
2. Put all of the ingredients in a bowl and mix gently to combine. Add avocado after the other ingredients have been combined. Serve the steak sliced with the bean mixture.

Nutritional Facts
Calories: 328 Kcal Proteins: 31 g Fats: 11 g Carbs: 25 g

5.17 Summer Garden Fish Tacos

Prepping time: 20 mins, Cooking Time: 20 mins, Servings: 4

Ingredients

- 1 sweet corn, husk removed
- 1 poblano pepper, seeds removed
- 4 fillets tilapia
- 1/8 tsp. salt
- 1 yellow summer squash, halved lengthwise

- 1 chopped tomato
- 1/3 cup red onion, chopped
- 3 tbsp. fresh cilantro, coarsely chopped
- 1 tsp. lime zest, grated
- 3 tbsp. lime juice
- 8 taco shells, warmed
- ½ avocado, sliced and peeled

Directions

1. Coat the grill rack lightly with oil. Covered, pepper & grill corn until softened, 10 to 12 mins, turning periodically. Allow cooling slightly. Then season fish with salt. Covered, grill the fish and squash over medium flame until the fish starts to flake readily using a fork and the squash is cooked, 7-9 mins, rotating once.
2. Remove the corn kernels off the cob and put them in a basin. Pepper and squash should be chopped and added to the corn. Combine lime juice, cilantro, tomato, onion, and lime zest in a medium bowl. Top fish taco shells with avocado slices and corn mixture.

Nutritional Facts
Calories: 278 Kcal Proteins: 25 g Fats: 10 g Carbs: 26 g

5.18 Tuna with Tuscan White Bean Salad

Prepping time: 20 mins, Cooking Time: 10 mins, Servings: 2

Ingredients

- 1 can cannellini beans, drained and rinsed
- 3 finely chopped celery ribs
- 1 red pepper, chopped
- 1 finely chopped plum tomato, seeded
- 1/2 cup basil leaves, thinly sliced
- 1/4 cup red onion, finely chopped
- 3 tbsp. olive oil
- 2 tbsp. vinegar red wine
- 1 tbsp. lemon juice
- 1/4 tsp. salt
- 1/4 tsp. pepper

Tuna:

- 4 tuna steaks
- 1 tbsp. olive oil
- 1/4 tsp. salt
- 1/4 tsp. pepper

Directions

1. In a mixing basin, whisk together the first six ingredients. Whisk together the pepper, oil, salt, vinegar, and lemon juice in another bowl. Distribute evenly on bean mixture; mix to coat. Refrigerate until ready to serve.
2. Oil the tuna with the brush. Season with pepper and salt and arrange on a well-greased grill rack. Cover and cook over a high flame until the center is slightly pink for 3 to 4 mins on both sides. Serve alongside salad.

Nutritional Facts:
Calories: 409 Kcal Proteins: 45 g Fats: 16 g Carbs: 20 g

5.19 Chicken & Goat Cheese Skillet

Prepping time: 15 mins, Cooking Time: 15 mins, Servings: 2

Ingredients

- ½ lb. chicken breasts, boneless and skinless, 1-inch pieces
- 1/4 tsp. salt
- 1/8 tsp. pepper
- 2 tsp. olive oil
- 1 cup asparagus, cut fresh
- 1 minced garlic clove
- 3 chopped plum tomatoes,
- 3 tbsp. milk
- 2 tbsp. goat cheese, herbed fresh, crumbled
- Rice or pasta, cooked
- Goat cheese

Directions

1. Season chicken with pepper to taste. Sauté chicken in a medium pan on medium-high flame until no longer pink, 4 to 6 mins. Take out of the pan and set it aside to keep it heated.
2. Mix asparagus to pan; cook and continue stirring on a medium flame for 1 min. Add tomatoes, 2 tbsp. cheese and milk; simmer, covered, over medium flame for 2-3 mins, or until cheese starts to melt. Combine with chicken. Serve alongside rice. Additional cheese, if desired, may be sprinkled on top.

Nutritional Facts:
Calories: 251 Kcal Fats: 11 g Carbs: 8 g Proteins: 29 g

5.20 Shrimp Orzo with Feta

Prepping time: 25 mins, Cooking Time: 20 mins, Serve: 4

Ingredients

- 1 1/4 cups orzo pasta
- 2 tbsp. olive oil
- 2 minced garlic cloves
- 2 medium chopped tomatoes
- 2 tbsp. lemon juice
- 1 1/4 lb. shrimp, peeled
- 2 tbsp. minced cilantro
- 1/4 tsp. pepper
- 1/2 cup feta cheese, crumbled

Directions

1. Make orzo pasta according per the package directions. Then over medium flame heat oil in a pan. Continue cooking for 1 min. Lemon juice and tomatoes are optional. Bring to a boil over high heat. Incorporate shrimp. Cook it on low heat, covered, for 4-5 mins, or till shrimp become pink.
2. Heat orzo, pepper and cilantro into shrimp mixture. Garnish with feta cheese, if desired.

Nutritional Facts:
Calories: 406 Kcal Fats: 12 g Carbs: 40 g Proteins: 33 g

5.21 Savory Braised Chicken with Vegetables

Prepping time: 15 mins, Cook Time: 40 mins, Serve: 6

Ingredients

- 1/2 cup breadcrumbs
- 6 chicken breast halves, boneless and skinless
- 2 tbsp. olive oil
- 1 can beef broth
- 2 tbsp. tomato paste
- 1 tsp. poultry seasoning
- 1/2 tsp. salt
- 1/2 tsp. pepper
- 1 lb. baby carrots
- 1 lb. mushrooms, sliced fresh
- 2 zucchinis, sliced
- Baguette, sliced (optional)

Directions

1. In a small dish, combine breadcrumbs. Coat each side of chicken breasts with breadcrumbs; brush off the extra.
2. Cook chicken in batches, 2 to 4 mins each side, or till browned. Take chicken out of the pan.
3. In the same pan, combine tomato paste, broth, and spices; simmer on a medium-high flame, continue stirring to remove browned pieces from the bottom of the pan. Bring to the veggies and chicken. Now cook it at low heat, covered, for 25 to 30 mins, or till veggies are soft and a thermometer placed into the chicken registers 165°F. Serve with an additional baguette, if preferred.

Nutritional Fact
Calories: 247 Kcal Fats: 8 g Carbs: 16 g Proteins: 28 g

5.22 Garlic Tilapia with Spicy Kale

Prepping time: 20 mins, Cooking Time: 15 mins, Servings: 4

Ingredients

- 3 tbsp. olive oil
- 2 minced garlic cloves
- 1 tsp. fennel seed
- 1/2 tsp. red pepper, crushed
- 1 bunch kale, coarsely chopped
- 2/3 cup water
- 4 fillets tilapia
- 3/4 tsp. pepper, divided
- 1/2 tsp. garlic salt
- 1 can cannellini beans, drained and rinsed
- 1/2 tsp. salt

Directions

1. Heat 1 tbsp. oil in a 6-quart stockpot over medium flame. Cook and stir for 1 min with the fennel, garlic, and pepper flakes. Bring greens and water to a boil. Cover it at low heat cook for 10 to 12 mins or till kale is tender.
2. In the meanwhile, season the fish using 1/2 tsp. pepper and 1/4 tsp. garlic salt. Heat oil on medium heat in the skillet. Cook 3 to 4 mins on both sides or until tilapia starts to flake readily with a fork.

3. Toss the kale with the beans, remaining pepper and salt; cook through, turning regularly. Serve alongside tilapia.

Nutritional Facts
Calories: 359 Kcal Fats: 13 g Carbs: 24 g Proteins: 39 g

5.23 Chicken Tacos with Avocado Salsa

Prepping time: 30 mins, Cooking Time: 10 mins, Servings: 4

Ingredients

- 1lb. chicken breasts, boneless and skinless
- 1/3 cup water
- 1 tsp. sugar
- 1 tbsp. chili powder
- 1 tsp. onion powder
- 1 tsp. dried oregano
- 1 tsp. ground cumin
- 1 tsp. paprika
- 1/2 tsp. salt
- 1/2 tsp. garlic powder
- 1 cubed avocado
- 1 cup frozen corn, thawed
- 1 cup cherry tomatoes, quartered
- 2 tsp. lime juice
- 8 warmed taco shells

Directions

1. On a medium-high flame, heat nonstick skillet sprayed with cooking oil. Brown the chicken. Then add the sugar, spices and water. Cook them for 4 to 5 mins or till chicken is no longer pink and stir periodically. In the meanwhile, carefully combine corn, avocado, lime juice and tomatoes in a small bowl. Fill taco shells halfway with the chicken mix; top with avocado salsa.
2. "In the freezer" option: Put in the freezer meat mixture inserted in containers for the freezer. To use it: defrost partly in the refrigerator. In a saucepan, heat the mixture, stirring periodically and adding a splash of water if required.

Nutritional Facts
Calories: 354 Kcal Fats: 15 g Carbs: 30 g Proteins: 27 g

5.24 Healthy Tuscan Chicken

Prepping time: 25 mins, Cooking Time: 15 mins, Servings: 4

Ingredients

- 4 chicken breasts, boneless and skinless
- 1/4 tsp. pepper
- 2 tbsp. olive oil
- 1 red, green, and yellow pepper
- 2 thin sliced pieces deli ham, chopped
- 2 minced garlic cloves
- 1 can tomatoes, undrained
- 1/4 cup chicken broth

- 2 tbsp. minced basil
- 1 tsp. minced oregano

Directions

1. Season chicken well with pepper. Brown the chicken in oil in a nonstick pan. Remove from heat and keep warm. Sauté prosciutto and peppers in the same pan until peppers become soft. Put garlic and cook it for an additional 1 min.
2. Combine tomatoes, chicken, broth, basil and oregano in a medium bowl. Bring it to boil at high heat. At low heat cover and cook it for 12 to 15 mins, till a thermometer registers 170°F.

Nutritional Fact:
Calories: 304 Kcal Fats: 12 g Carbs: 11 g Proteins: 38 g

5.25 Spicy Turkey Tenderloin

Prepping time: 20 mins, Cooking Time: 25mins, Servings: 2

Ingredients

- 1/2 tsp. chili powder
- 1/2 tsp. ground cumin
- 1/2 tsp. salt
- 1/8 tsp. cayenne pepper
- 1 tenderloin turkey breast
- 3 tsp. olive oil, divided
- 1/4 cup chicken broth
- 2 tbsp. lime juice
- 3 tbsp. chopped onion
- 2 tbsp. jalapeno pepper, chopped
- 1 cup black beans, drained and rinsed
- 1/2 cup frozen corn
- 3 tbsp. chopped tomato
- 4 tsp. Picante sauce
- 1 tbsp. minced fresh cilantro
- 2 lime wedges

Directions

1. Combine the cayenne pepper, chili powder, salt, and cumin in a mixing bowl. Distribute half of the spice mixture evenly on the turkey. Brown the turkey in a pan with 2 tbsp. oil for 3 to 4 mins on both sides. In a skillet, combine lime juice and broth. At low heat cover and simmer, stirring once, till turkey juices flow clear and thermometer reaches 170°F, 15-18 mins.
2. In a pan, heat the leftover oil and sauté the jalapeño and onion until crunchy. Transfer the mixture to a bowl. Combine the beans, Picante sauce, corn, tomato, cilantro, and the rest of the spice mix in a medium bowl. Turkey should be served with lime wedges and salsa.

Nutritional Facts:
Calories: 342 Kcal Fats: 9 g Carbs: 32 g Proteins: 35 g

5.26 Artichoke Ratatouille Chicken

Prepping time: 25 mins, Cooking Time: 60 mins, Servings: 6

Ingredients

- 3 Japanese eggplants
- 4 plum tomatoes
- 1 sweet yellow pepper
- 1 red sweet pepper
- 1 onion
- 1 can artichoke hearts
- 2 tbsp. fresh thyme
- 2 tbsp. capers
- 2 tbsp. olive oil
- 2 cloves garlic
- 1 tsp. Creole seasoning
- 1 1/2 lb. boneless chicken breasts
- 1 cup white wine
- 1/4 cup Asiago cheese

Directions

1. Set the oven to 350°F. Transfer eggplants, onion, tomatoes, and peppers to a bowl. Combine artichokes, thyme, 1/2 teaspoon of Creole spice, capers, garlic and oil in a medium bowl.
2. Season chicken with the remainder of the Creole spice. Move chicken onto a 13 by 9-inch baking dish sprayed with cooking oil, cover with the vegetable mix. Vegetables should be drizzled with wine.
3. Bake for 30 mins, covered. Uncover and bake for an additional 30 to 45 minutes, or till chicken is no longer pink and veggies are soft. Sprinkle cheese on top. Serve with spaghetti, if preferred.

Nutritional Facts:
Calories: 252 Kcal Fats: 9 g Carbs: 15 g Proteins: 28 g

5.27 Asian Lettuce Wraps

Prepping time: 10 mins, Cooking Time: 15 mins, Servings: 4

Ingredients

- 1 tbsp. canola oil
- 1 lb. ground turkey, lean
- 1 jalapeno pepper
- 2 thinly sliced green onions
- 2 garlic cloves
- 2 tbsp. fresh basil
- 2 tbsp. lime juice
- 2 tbsp. soy sauce
- 1 to 2 tbsp. chili garlic sauce
- 1 tbsp. sugar
- 12 Bibb
- 1 julienned cucumber
- 1 julienned carrot
- 2 cups bean sprouts

Directions

1. Put the oil on medium flame in a pan. Cook for 6 to 8 mins, or till the turkey is no longer pink, crumbling it. Add the jalapeo, garlic, and green onions and cook for an additional 2 minutes.
2. Combine basil, chili garlic sauce, lime juice, sugar and soy sauce in a medium saucepan; bring to a boil.
3. Lettuce should be folded over the filling.

Nutritional Facts:
Calories: 259 Kcal Fats: 12 g Carbs: 12 g Proteins: 26 g

5.28 Grilled Jerk Shrimp Orzo Salad

Prepping time: 25 mins, Cooking Time: 10 mins, Servings:

Ingredients

- 1/3 cup uncooked orzo pasta
- 1/2 lb. uncooked shrimp
- 1 tbsp. Caribbean jerk seasoning
- 1 ear sweet corn, husked
- 1 tsp. olive oil
- 6 trimmed asparagus spears
- 1 sweet red chopped pepper

Dressing

- 3 tbsp. lime juice
- 1 tbsp. water
- 1 tbsp. olive oil
- 1/8 tsp. salt
- 1/8 tsp. pepper

Directions

1. Prepare orzo as directed on the packet. Using cold water, thoroughly rinse and then pat dry. Thread shrimp and jerk spice onto wooden skewers and serve immediately. Coat the corn cobs with a thin coating of oil.
2. Cook the corn till tender and gently browned, 10 to 12 mins above-covered grill on medium flame, turning once; cook the asparagus till crunchy, 5 to 7 mins. Grill the shrimp until they become pink, 1 to 2 mins on each side.
3. Discard cob of corn and cut the asparagus into 1-inch sections. Remove the shrimp from the skewer. Combine orzo with shrimp, grilled veggies and red pepper in a dish to blend. Toss the salad with the dressing after whisking up the ingredients.

Nutritional Facts:
Calories: 340 Kcal Fats: 12 g Carbs: 35 g Proteins: 25 g

5.29 Dee's Grilled Tuna with Greens

Prepping time: 10 mins, Cooking Time: 20 mins, Servings: 4

Ingredients

- 1 lb. tuna steaks
- 2 tsp. olive oil
- 1/4 tsp. salt
- 1/4 tsp. pepper
-
- 6 cups baby spinach
- 1 cup grape tomatoes
- 3/4 cup shelled edamame, frozen
- 1/2 cup frozen corn

Citrus Vinaigrette:

- 2 tbsp. olive oil
- 1 tbsp. fresh basil
- 1 tbsp. wine vinegar
- 1 tbsp. honey
- 1 tbsp. lime juice
- 1 tbsp. lemon juice
- 1 tbsp. orange juice
- 1/8 tsp. salt
- 1/8 tsp. pepper

Directions

1. Wet a paper towel with a little frying oil before applying it to the grill rack with the long-handled tongs. After that, use the olive oil and brush the tuna and add pepper and salt to taste. Cook for 2 to 3 mins on both sides on a covered grill or broil 3 to 4 inches from the fire. Cook for more time if you desire. Allow standing for a minimum of five mins before using.
2. Meanwhile, mix spinach, edamame, tomatoes, and corn in a bowl, then set aside. Combine vinaigrette ingredients in the bowl before pouring over salad and tossing to combine.
3. Serve salad on four plates and top with sliced tuna. Prepare the food and serve it right away.

Nutritional Facts:
Calories: 294 Kcal Fats: 12 g Carbs: 16 g Proteins: 32 g

5.30 Lemon-Lime Salmon with Veggie Sauté

Prepping time: 10 mins, Cooking Time: 20 mins, Servings: 6

Ingredients

- 6 salmon fillets
- 1/2 cup lemon juice
- 1/2 cup lime juice
- 1 tsp. seafood seasoning
- 1/4 tsp. salt
- 2 sweet red sliced peppers
- 2 sweet yellow sliced peppers
- 1 large red sliced onion
- 2 tsp. olive oil
- 1 package thawed frozen corn
- 2 cups portobello mushrooms
- 2 cups cut asparagus
- 2 tbsp. fresh tarragon

Directions

1. Add the lime and lemon juice to the salmon on a baking dish. Season with salt and seafood seasoning before serving. Bake uncovered at 425°F for 10 t0 15 mins, just until the fish flakes quickly when tested with a fork.
2. Peppers and onions should be sauteed in the oil for three minutes in a pan sprayed with cooking spray. Cook and stir the corn, mushrooms, and asparagus for 3 to 4 more mins, or until they are done. Add the asparagus at the end of the cooking time. Tarragon may be added at this point if desired. Serving suggestion: Pair with a piece of salmon.

Nutritional Facts:
Calories: 329 Kcal Fats: 15 g Carbs: 25 g Proteins: 27 g

5.31 Refreshing Shrimp Salad

Prepping time: 15 mins, Cooking Time: 0 mins, Servings: 4

Ingredients

- 1 package mixed salad
- 1 lb. cooked shrimp
- 1 navel orange
- 1 chopped ripe avocado
- 1 cup fresh strawberries
- 1/2 cup green onions, thinly sliced
- Salad dressing

Directions

1. Arrange shrimp, salad greens, avocado, orange, onions and strawberries on each of four dishes for serving. Dress the dish.

Nutritional Facts:
Calories: 239 Kcal Fats: 9 g Carbs: 16 g Proteins: 25 g

5.32 Savory Pork Salad

Prepping time: 10 mins, Cooking Time: 15 mins, Servings: 2

Ingredients

- 1 garlic clove
- 1/2 tsp. fresh ginger root
- 2 tsp. olive oil
- 1/2 lb. thinly sliced pork tenderloin
- 2 tsp. brown sugar
- 2 tsp. fresh basil
- 2 tsp. soy sauce
- 1 1/2 tsp. lime juice
- 1 1/2 tsp. water
- 1 tsp. fresh oregano
- 3 cups torn mixture of salad greens
- 1/2 cup grape tomatoes
- 1/2 sliced red onion
- 1/2 sweet yellow chili

Directions

1. In a large skillet over medium heat, sauté the ginger and garlic for 30 seconds with the oil. Cook and stir the pork till it no longer has a pink hue to it. Set aside but keep it warm.
2. In the same skillet, combine brown sugar, lime juice, basil, and soy sauce.
3. Assemble the ingredients and bring them to a rapid boil. After several mins, turn off the flame and let the dish settle for a while. Combine the onions, greens, pork, and yellow pepper in the salad bowl. The dressing should be served shortly after being drizzled over the salad.

Nutritional Facts:
Calories: 229 Kcal Fats: 9 g Carbs: 13 g Proteins: 25 g

5.33 Cobb Salad Wraps

Prepping time: 10 mins, Cooking Time: 5 mins, Servings: 4

Ingredients

- 2 cups cooked breast chicken
- 1/2 cup chopped avocado
- 4 cooked and crumbled bacon strips
- 1 thinly sliced celery rib
- 1 sliced green onion
- 2 tbsp. ripe olives, chopped
- 2 tbsp. crumbled cheese
- 2 tbsp. lemon juice
- 1 tbsp. honey
- 1 1/2 tsp. Dijon mustard
- 1 garlic clove
- 1/4 tsp. dill weed
- 1/4 tsp. salt
- 1/8 tsp. pepper
- 1 tbsp. olive oil
- 4 torn romaine leaves
- 4 whole wheat warmed tortillas
- 1 chopped tomato

Directions

1. Mix the cheese, chicken, avocado, bacon, onion, celery and olives in a bowl. Pour all of the ingredients into a separate dish except for the dill weed. Whisk in the oil until the mixture is smooth. Make a quick frying pan sauce with oil and the sauce, then add the chicken.
2. Add romaine and 2/3 cup of chicken mix to the tortilla and cover with a second tortilla layer. Cover the tomato with the tortilla once it has been rolled.

Nutritional Facts:
Calories: 372 Kcal Fats: 14 g Carbs: 32 g Proteins: 29 g

5.34 Pork Grapefruit Stir-Fry

Prepping time: 10 mins, Cooking Time: 15 mins, Servings: 6

Ingredients

- 3 tbsp. cornstarch
- 3/4 cup of juice of thawed grapefruit concentrate
- 3/4 cup water
- 3 tbsp. soy sauce
- 1 tbsp. honey
- 1/2 tsp. ground ginger
- 3 cups sliced zucchini
- 1 sweet red chili
- 1 tbsp. canola oil
- 1 1/2 lb. pork tenderloin
- 3 medium grapefruits
- 1 tbsp. toasted sesame seeds

Directions

1. Mix the concentrated grapefruit juice, cornstarch, soy sauce, water, ginger and honey in a dish and place it in the refrigerator to thicken. Stir-fry the red pepper and zucchini in the oil in a pan or wok for 3 to 4 mins, or till crisp and tender.

2. Warm-up by removing and storing in a warm place. Put 1/2 of the meat and cook for 4 mins or till no longer pink. Warm-up by removing and storing in a warm place. Continue with the rest of the pork.
3. Bring sauce to the pan to boil after adding it. Cook and whisk for 2 mins or till thickened. Stir the pork and veggies until they are well-coated before returning them to the pan. Add grapefruit and gently mix. Sesame seeds may be used as a finishing touch. If you'd like, you may also serve this dish with rice.

Nutritional Facts:
Calories: 320 Kcal Fats: 7g Carbs: 39 g Proteins: 27 g

5.35 Beef Brunch Bake

Prepping time: 15 mins, Cooking Time: 60 mins, Servings: 8

Ingredients

- 8 slices cubed bread
- 3 cups beef broth
- 4 cups cubed cooked beef
- 1/2 cup instant rice uncooked
- 1/2 cup pimientos diced
- 2 tbsp. fresh parsley, minced
- 1/2 tsp. salt (optional)
- 4 large beaten eggs

Directions

1. Toss bread pieces and broth in the bowl and add rice, beef, parsley and pimientos Place in a 13 by 9-inch oiled baking dish. Pour the beaten eggs over everything.
2. Bake for 60 mins at 325°F, uncovered, till a knife placed in the middle comes out cleanly.

Nutritional Facts:
Calories: 233 Kcal Fats: 6 g Carbs: 18 g Proteins: 27 g

5.36 Cod with Hearty Tomato Sauce

Prepping time: 20 mins, Cooking Time: 10 mins, Servings: 4

Ingredients

- 2 cans diced tomatoes with basil, oregano and garlic
- 4 cod fillets
- 2 tbsp. olive oil
- 2 thinly sliced onions
- 1/2 tsp. dried oregano
- 1/4 tsp. pepper
- 1/4 tsp. pepper flakes, crushed
- Hot cooked pasta
- Minced parsley

Directions

1. Blend the tomatoes till smooth. Put the cover on and blend until smooth.

2. Use paper towels to remove excess moisture from fish. Heat 1 tbsp. oil on a medium-high flame in the pan. Add the cod fillets and cook for 2 to 4 mins from each side, or until the fish is just starting to color up the surface. Take it out of the pan and set it aside.
3. The remaining oil should be heated to a medium-high flame in the same skillet. Add the onions, then simmer, often stirring, for 2 to 4 mins, or once they are soft. Bring to a boil, then add the spices and pureed tomatoes.
4. Add the fish and bring the sauce back to a boil, then serve with a spoonful of sauce on top. The goal is to reduce the heat and simmer until the salmon flakes readily with the fork, around 5 to 7 mins. Serve this dish with pasta, if desired. Add some fresh parsley if you want.

Nutritional Facts:
Calories: 271 Kcal Fats: 8 g Carbs: 17 g Proteins: 29 g

5.37 Spicy Coconut Shrimp with Quinoa

Prepping time: 20 mins, Cooking Time: 20 mins, Servings: 4

Ingredients

- 1 cup quinoa
- 2 cups water
- 1/4 tsp. salt

Shrimp:

- 1 tsp. olive oil
- 1 chopped onion
- 1 tbsp. fresh ginger root
- 1/2 tsp. curry powder
- 1/2 tsp. ground cumin
- 1/4 tsp. salt
- 1/4 tsp. cayenne pepper
- 1 lb. uncooked shrimp
- 2 cups snow peas
- 3 tbsp. coconut milk
- 1 tbsp. orange juice
- 1/4 cup sweetened shredded toasted coconut
- 1/4 cup fresh cilantro

Directions

1. Boil quinoa, salt and water in a large pot. Cook for 12 to 15 mins, covered, over low heat till water is absorbed. Remove from the heat and stir with just a fork until well-combined and fluffy.
2. At the same time, heat the oil in the big nonstick pan over medium flame. Add the onion and simmer for 4 to 6 mins, often stirring, until soft. Continue to heat for another min after adding the curry powder, ginger, nutmeg, cayenne and salt.
3. Stir-fry shrimp and snow peas for 3 to 4 mins, or until shrimp is pink and snow peas become crisp-tender. Bring the coconut milk, orange juice, and honey to a boil, and continue to cook until well heated. Top each plate with cilantro and coconut, and do not serve without quinoa.

Nutritional Facts:
Calories: 330 Kcal Fats: 8 g Carbs: 37 g Proteins: 26 g

5.38 Zippy Turkey Zoodles

Prepping time: 25 mins, Cooking Time: 20 mins, Servings: 4

Ingredients

- 4 tsp. olive oil
- 1 lb. ground turkey
- 1 chopped onion
- 1 chopped jalapeno pepper
- 2 garlic cloves
- 3/4 tsp. ground cumin
- 1/2 tsp. salt
- 1/4 tsp. chili powder
- 1/4 tsp. crushed pepper flakes
- 1/4 tsp. pepper
- 3 zucchinis
- 4 plum tomatoes, chopped
- 1 cup frozen corn
- 1 cup black beans

Directions

1. Heat 2 tsp. olive oil in a nonstick pan on medium flame. Mix jalapeno, turkey, garlic and onion and cook for 8 to 10 mins, until the turkey is no longer pink, breaking up the turkey into crumbs, and the veggies are cooked. Drain. Turn the heat off and cover it so that it remain warm. Clean the pan with a damp cloth.
2. Cook zucchini for about 3 mins in the same skillet with the leftover oil. Zucchini should be crisp-tender. Add the remaining turkey mix and the tomatoes, beans and corn, and cook through. If preferred, top with cheese and cilantro.

Nutritional Facts
Calories: 332 Kcal Fats: 14 g Carbs: 26 g Proteins: 29 g

5.39 Hearty Chicken Gyros

Prepping time: 30 mins, Cooking Time: 5 mins, Servings: 6

Ingredients

- 1 1/2 lb. boneless chicken breasts
- 1/2 cup lemon-pepper marinade
- 3 tbsp. minced fresh mint

Sauce

- 1/2 cup Greek yogurt
- 2 tbsp. lemon juice
- 1 tsp. dill weed
- 1/2 tsp. garlic powder

Assembly

- 1 chopped cucumber
- 1 chopped tomato
- 1/4 cup of onion, chopped
- 6 whole wheat warmed pitas
- 1/3 cup crumbled feta

Directions

1. Take the chicken with the min and marinade in a small bowl until well-coated. Refrigerate, covered, for at least six hours before using.
2. Remove chicken from marinade and dry with paper towels on a medium-high flame; heat a big nonstick pan. Cook and stir the chicken for 4 to 6 mins, or until it is no longer pink.
3. Put all the sauce ingredients to a bowl and mix them together. and set aside. Cucumber, onion and tomato are placed in another dish. Serve pita pockets filled with chicken, sauce, cheese and vegetables.

Nutritional Facts
Calories: 248 Kcal Fats: 4 g Carbs: 22 g Proteins: 30 g

5.40 Tuscan Fish Packets

Prepping time: 15 mins, Cooking Time: 15 mins, Servings: 4

Ingredients

- 1 can northern beans
- 4 chopped plum tomatoes
- 1 chopped zucchini
- 1 chopped onion
- 1 garlic clove
- 1/4 cup white wine
- 3/4 tsp. salt
- 1/4 tsp. pepper
- 4 tilapia fillets
- 1 thin slice of lemon

Directions

1. Set the oven to 400°F. Put all the ingredients to a large bowl and mix well. Season with salt and pepper to taste.
2. Pat dry the fish after rinsing it. Fillets should be placed on a foil sheet that is 18 by 12 inches and season with the remaining pepper and salt. Top with lemon wedges and bean mix. To seal, fold the foil over the fish and crimp the edges. Place the packets on a baking sheet and bake for 20 mins.
3. Bake the fish and veggies for 15 to 20 mins, or till fish and veggies are just starting to flake readily when tested with a fork.

Nutritional Facts
Calories: 270 Kcal Fats: 2 g Carbs: 23 g Proteins: 38 g

5.41 Slow-Cooked Italian Chicken

Prepping time: 20 mins, Cooking Time: 4 hours, Servings: 4

Ingredients

- 4 boneless chicken breast halves
- 1 can chicken broth
- 1 can stewed tomatoes
- 1 can tomato sauce
- 1 chopped green pepper
- 1 chopped green onion
- 1 garlic clove
- 3 tsp. chili powder
- 1 tsp. ground mustard
- 1/2 tsp. pepper
- 1/4 tsp. garlic powder
- 1/4 tsp. onion powder
- 1/3 cup flour
- 1/2 cup cold water
- Pasta, cooked

Directions

1. Put the chicken in the 3-quart slow cooker, set it on low heat; add the broth mixture. Stir in the tomatoes, garlic, onion and seasonings over chicken. Cover & cook for 4 to 5 hours or until meat is cooked and tender. Keep chicken warm by removing it from the pan and placing it in the oven.
2. Mix cooking fluids and transfer to a large pot, skim fat. Stir together the flour, sugar and cold water until smooth. Add juices & boil. Cook for 2 mins and stir constantly. Serve with spaghetti and chicken. If preferred, sprinkle with more basil and parmesan before serving.

Nutritional Facts:
Calories: 231 Kcal Fats: 3 g Carbs: 22 g Proteins: 28 g

5.42 Chicken with Celery Root Puree

Prepping time: 30 mins, Cooking Time: 15 mins, Servings: 4

Ingredients

- 4 boneless chicken breast halves
- 1/2 tsp. pepper
- 1/4 tsp. salt
- 3 tsp. canola oil
- 1 large, chopped celery root
- 2 cups chopped squash, peeled butternut
- 1 chopped onion
- 2 garlic cloves
- 2/3 cup juice of unsweetened apple

Directions

1. Season the chicken with salt and pepper. Heat 2 tsp. oil in the nonstick pan sprayed with cooking spray. Cook the chicken until it's golden brown on both sides. Set the chicken aside after removing it from the pan.
2. Put the remaining oil in a medium-sized saucepan at heat, until it shimmers. Cook and stir till the squash seem crisp-tender, then add the celery root, onion and squash. Cook for a further min after adding the garlic.

3. Pour apple juice and chicken back to the pan. Bring the mixture to a rolling boil. At low heat simmer the chicken for 12 to 15 mins, till it reaches to a temperature of 165°Farhienhiet when tested with a thermometer.
4. Remove the chicken and keep it warm in a pan covered with aluminum foil. Allow the vegetable mix to cool gently before serving. Using a blender, puree the mixture until it's smooth. Put the chicken back in the pan and reheat until hot. Serve it with chicken to make it a meal.

Nutritional Facts:
Calories: 328 Kcal Fats: 8 g Carbs: 28 g Proteins: 37 g

5.43 Tuscan Chicken and Beans

Prepping time: 15 mins, Cooking Time: 15 mins, Servings: 4

Ingredients

- 1 lb. boneless chicken breasts
- 2 tsp. minced rosemary
- 1/4 tsp. salt
- 1/4 tsp. ground pepper
- 1 cup chicken broth
- 2 tbsp. chopped tomatoes
- 1 can cannellini beans

Directions

1. Whisk the chicken, salt, pepper and rosemary in a small bowl. Cook chicken till browned in skillet sprayed with cooking spray.
2. Using a rubber spatula, scrape off any browned pieces from the bottom of the pan and add to the sauce. Bring the mixture to a rolling boil. Cook, covered, for 3 to 5 mins till the chicken is tender, and liquid runs clear. Cook the beans, occasionally stirring, until heated through.

Nutritional Facts:
Calories: 216 Kcal Fats: 3 g Carbs: 17 g Proteins: 28 g

5.44 The Ultimate Fish Tacos

Prepping time: 20 mins, Cooking Time: 10 mins, Servings: 6

Ingredients

- 1/4 cup olive oil
- 1 tsp. ground cardamom
- 1 tsp. paprika
- 1 tsp. salt
- 1 tsp. pepper
- 6 Mahi fillets
- 12 corn tortillas
- 2 cups red cabbage, chopped
- 1 cup fresh cilantro, chopped
- Salsa verde

- 2 limes
- Hot pepper sauce

Direction

1. Assemble the first five ingredients in a bowl and mix it in a 13 by 9-inch baking dish.. Turn to coat the fillets after adding them. Leave for 30 mins in the refrigerator with the lid on.
2. Remove fish from the marinade and set aside to drain. Cook mahi-mahi, covered, on the oiled grill, on medium-high heat for 4 to 5 mins on each side, till it flakes readily with a fork. Take the fish out of the equation.Grill the tortillas for 30 to 45 seconds, depending on their size, on the grill rack.Stay as warm as possible.
3. Add fish to tortillas and top with red cabbage, salsa verde and cilantro, if preferred. Fold the tortilla over the fish mix and serve with lime and spicy pepper sauce, if desired. Serve with an extra dash of hot sauce and lime wedges.

Nutritional Facts:
Calories: 284 Kcal Fats: 5 g Carbs: 26 g Proteins: 35 g

5.45 Indian Baked Chicken

Prepping time: 15 mins, Cooking Time: 60 mins, Servings: 6

Ingredients

- 1 lb. red potatoes
- 4 medium carrots
- 1 large onion
- 6 boneless chicken thighs
- 1 can chicken broth
- 1 can tomato paste
- 2 tbsp. olive oil
- 1 tbsp. ground turmeric
- 1 tsp. chili powder
- 1 tsp. ground cumin
- 1/2 tsp. salt
- 1/2 tsp. garlic powder
- 1/2 tsp. pepper

Directions

1. Place the vegetables, potatoes, onion and carrot in greased 13 by 9-inch baking dish. Add chicken. The other ingredients should be mixed in a separate dish and then poured over the top.
2. A thermometer put into the chicken should read 180°F for baking and the veggies must be tender.

Nutritional Facts
Calories: 323 Kcal Fats: 13 g Carbs: 25 g Proteins: 25 g

Chapter 6: Dinner Recipes

6.1 Mediterranean low carb broccoli salad

Prepping time: 25 mins, Cooking time: 25 mins, servings: 1

Ingredients

For the salad:

- 5 cups broccoli
- 1/2 cup artichoke hearts, sliced and cooked in oil
- 1/2 cup tomatoes, cooked in oil
- 1/2 cup olives
- 1/3 cup red onion
- 1/4 cup sunflower seeds

For the dressing:

- 2 cups of Greek yogurt
- Zest and juice of one lemon
- 4 1/2 tsp. monk fruit
- 3/4 tsp. dried oregano
- 1/2 tsp. garlic
- 1/2 tsp. ground basil
- 1/2 tsp. ground thyme
- 1 tsp. sea salt
- Pepper
- 2 tbsp. sun-dried tomato oil

Direction:
1. Stir all salad ingredients together in a large mixing bowl.
2. Combine all dressing items in a large bowl and whisk until well combined.
3. Stir broccoli in sauce to ensure it is well-coated. To allow the broccoli to soak in the dressing and develop its flavor, cover, and chill for at least 2 hours or up to overnight.
4. Devour!

Nutritional facts:
Calories: 182 Kcal proteins: 5.9 g fats: 4.6 g carbs: 14.7 g

6.2 Chicken veggies stir fry

Prepping time: 30 mins, Cooking time: 30 mins, servings: 4

Ingredients

- 2 tbsp. soy sauce, reduced sodium
- 1 tbsp. minced ginger
- Juice of one lime
- 2 tsp. sesame oil
- 1 lb. sliced or diced boneless chicken
- 1 tbsp. canola oil
- A couple of carrots, thinly sliced
- 2 cups broccoli florets
- A medium zucchini cut in half and then into half-moons around a quarter-inch thick
- 4 cloves garlic
- A couple of green onions, roughly chopped
- 1 seeded and minced jalapeno pepper
- ¼ cup sliced basil
- ¼ cup chopped cilantro
- Brown rice

Directions

1. In a large dish, mix soy sauce, sesame oil, ginger, and lime juice. Place chicken in a zip-top bag, seal, and place in refrigerator for at least one hour or up to one day.
2. When you're prepared to make your stir fry, heat the oil in a large wok or nonstick pan over high heat. Stir-fry the chicken with the marinade for one min after adding it to the pan.
3. Continue to stir-fry for a further 7 mins or until the chicken is cooked through and the veggies are crisp-tender.
4. Add the remaining 1 tbsp. lime juice, sesame oil and soy sauce, to the bowl. Stir to combine. Remove from heat. Add the cilantro and basil just before serving.
5. If necessary, serve with brown rice.

Nutritional facts:
Calories: 220 Kcal proteins: 26 g fats: 9 g carbs: 11 g

6.3 Ground turkey sweet potato skillet

Prepping time: 10 mins, Cooking time: 17 mins, servings: 4

Ingredients

- 2 tbsp. olive oil
- 1 lb. ground turkey
- 1 tsp. garlic clove
- ½ cup onions
- ½ cup yellow pepper
- 1 ½ cups sweet potato
- Salt and powdered black pepper
- ½ cup shredded cheese

Directions

1. Put olive oil in a large cast-iron pan over medium heat.
2. Garlic and ground turkey meat should be added now. As turkey cooks, use a spoon to split it up. Cook for 5 mins, stirring periodically.
3. Continue to cook onions and yellow peppers for several more mins until they are tender.
4. Add salt, pepper, sweet potato, and red pepper flakes.
5. Cook the sweet potatoes covered in the pan until they are fork-tender, about 30 mins. Don't forget to give the mixture a few stirs. If the sweet potatoes aren't cooking quickly enough, add a little extra olive oil or water.
6. Set oven to 400°F while sweet potatoes are cooking.
7. To melt the cheese, place the pan in the oven once the sweet potatoes are done.
8. Take the dish off from the oven after the cheese has melted and top with fresh parsley.

Nutritional facts:
Calories: 250 Kcal proteins: 30 g fats: 15g carbs: 18 g

6.4 Vegetarian lentil tacos

Prepping time: 10 mins, cooking time: 3 hours 30 mins, servings: 9

Ingredients

- 1 ½ cups green lentils
- 3 cups vegetable broth
- 1 (10 oz) mild diced tomatoes and green chiles
- 1 tbsp. olive oil

- 1/2 cup crushed yellow onion
- 2 tsp. minced garlic
- 2 tsp. ground cumin
- 1 1/2 tsp. chili powder
- 1 1/2 tsp. ancho chili powder
- 1 tsp. paprika
- Salt and powdered black pepper for taste
- 3 tbsp. crushed fresh cilantro
- 1 tbsp. lime juice

Directions

1. In a 5-to-6-quart slow cooker, mix lentils, olive oil, garlic, tomatoes, broth, onions, chili powders, and paprika. Add a pinch of kosher salt and freshly ground black pepper for taste.
2. In a large pot, combine all ingredients and bring to a boil over high heat.
3. Add the cilantro and lime juice and mix well. Serve warm with additional toppings in warmed tortillas.

Nutritional facts
Calories: 145 Kcal proteins: 8 g fats: 2 g carbs: 23 g

6.5 Healthy general Tso's chicken

Prepping time: 25 mins, Cooking time: 10 mins, servings: 5

Ingredients

For the marinade

- 2 tsp. cornstarch
- 1/4 tsp. salt
- 1/8 tsp. powdered white pepper
- 2 boneless chicken breasts

For the sauce

- 1/4 cup tomato ketchup
- 2 tbsp. rice vinegar
- 4 tsp. hoisin sauce
- 4 tsp. brown sugar
- 4 tsp. soy sauce

For the stir-fry

- 2 tbsp. peanut oil
- One red chili (optional)
- 1 tsp. toasted sesame seeds
- 1 scallion, crushed

Directions

1. In a small bowl, mix cornstarch, white pepper, and salt. Toss the ingredients together and pour over the cut chicken. Set aside for 20 mins to marinate.

2. Then combine ketchup, brown sugar, rice vinegar, soy sauce, and hoisin sauce in a separate bowl and thoroughly mix. Reserve the sauce for later.
3. Heat a wok at medium-high heat and warm the peanut oil in it.
4. Stir-fry the chicken in batches for a few mins or until it's completely cooked and starting to brown.
5. The chili should be added, and then the sauce should be poured in. Stir the sauce into the chicken until it is well-coated.
6. Take the dish off from the heat and place it on a serving platter. To finish, sprinkle sesame seeds & scallion slices over the top.

Nutritional facts
Calories: 207 Kcal proteins: 12 g fats: 12 g carbs: 10 g

6.6 Banham chicken burger lettuce wraps

Prepping time: 10 mins, Cooking time: 10 mins, freezer time: 10 mins servings: 4

Ingredients

For the pickled vegetables

- ⅓ cup rice vinegar
- 1 tbsp. sugar
- 1 tsp. kosher salt
- ½ English cucumber, sliced
- 2 carrots, sliced

For the burgers

- 1 lb. chicken meat, ground
- 1 finely sliced scallion (2 tbsp)
- 1 tsp. grated ginger
- ½ tsp. minced garlic
- 1 tbsp. soy sauce
- Juice of 1/2 lime
- 1 tbsp. brown sugar

For serving

- Lettuce leaves

Directions

Make the pickled vegetables

1. In a small bowl, add vinegar, salt, and sugar and mix it. Add in the carrot, radish sticks, and cucumber and stir to combine. Allow at least ten mins for it to get to room temperature before using.
2. When you're ready to serve, remove the veggies from the water and drain completely.

Make the burgers

1. Mix ground chicken with scallions, brown sugar, garlic, lime juice, soy sauce, and ginger in a mixing bowl. Stir until well combined. Prepare plate according to your freezer and shape the mixture into four patties. For ten mins, place the dish in the freezer.
2. Cook for around 5 mins on each side, or until the internal temperature reaches 165°F. For those who don't have access to a grill, the broiler will do.

Serve

1. If necessary, top four big lettuce leaves with sriracha mayonnaise. Add a burger on the top of each serving.
2. If using jalapenos, add them now, along with the drained pickled veggies.

Nutritional facts:
Calories: 242 Kcal proteins: 23 g fats: 11 g carbs: 11 g

6.7 Lemon garlic salmon

Prepping time: 10 mins, Cooking time: 10 mins, servings: 4

Ingredients

- 1 ¼ lb. salmon filets
- 3 lemons, 2 squeezed and 1 sliced
- 2 tsp. lemon zest
- 4 cloves garlic
- 2 tbsp. olive oil
- 1 tsp. kosher salt
- 1/2 tsp. powdered black pepper
- Chopped parsley

Directions

1. Set oven to 400°F and drizzle some oil on a baking dish large enough to hold all of the salmon.
2. Toss together garlic, lemon juice, oil, and seasonings in a bowl. Put salmon fillets in a zip lock bag, and marinate.
3. Shut the bag and move it around a little to ensure the salmon pieces are uniformly covered with the marinade. Allow for a minimum of 30 mins of marinating time.
4. Then there is the preparation of the salmon: Put it on the upper side of the lemon segments, you just placed on a plate before doing this operation.
5. Bake the salmon for 12 to 15 mins in the oven, depending on how thick the fillet is.
6. Put a couple of lemon slices on the upper side of the cooked salmon, then turn the oven's broiler on. Cook for 3 mins under the broiler, or until the top is beautifully browned and crunchy.
7. Serve immediately after removing from oven & garnishing with parsley.

Nutritional facts:
Calories: 294 Kcal proteins: 29 g fats: 17 g carbs: 9 g

6.8 Summery tomato & zucchini quinoa pizza

Prepping time: 2 hours, cooking time: 25 mins, servings: 12

Ingredients

- 3/4 cup white quinoa soaked in three cups of water
- 1 sabra 10-ounce bottle and hummus with roasted red chilies
- 2 tbsp. water
- 1 tsp. baking powder
- 1/2 tsp. sea salt
- 1 zucchini
- 2 tomatoes
- 1 cup cheese
- Garnish with basil and roasted chili flakes that have been finely chopped

Directions

1. Quinoa should be soaked for two hours or ideally overnight in warm water.
2. Set oven to 425°F and prepare a cookie sheet along with parchment paper before you begin.
3. Then mix it all with 2 tbsp. of water, 1/4 cup of hummus, baking powder, and sea salt, then drain and rinse it again using a small mesh sieve. The thick batter will develop when the blender is run at high speed until it's completely smooth.
4. Spread the batter into a rectangle on a baking sheet coated with parchment paper using a spatula. Make the crust as thin as possible, no more than 1/8".
5. Bake for 10 mins on the middle rack, then turn the crust over and bake for an additional 8 mins.
6. Slice zucchini and tomatoes into pieces, whereas crust is baking.
7. The crust should be taken out of the oven, and the remaining hummus should be spread out evenly on a baking sheet (this will be used as the "sauce"). To serve, pile zucchini and tomato slices on top of the pesto sauce. Sprinkle with cheese and serve.
8. After the cheese has liquefied and the veggies are heated, bake for an additional 6 to 10 mins.
9. Slice into squares after removing from the oven. To serve, top with basil and chopped red pepper flakes and toss well.

Nutritional facts
Calories: 150 Kcal proteins: 4 g fats: 10 g carbs: 13 g

6.9 Mexican chopped salad

Prepping time: 25 mins, Cooking time: 25 mins, servings: 8

Ingredients

Ingredients for the dressing:

- ¼ cup lime juice
- 2 tbsp. honey
- ½ tsp. cumin
- 1 clove garlic
- ½ tsp. salt
- 2 tbsp. canola oil
- 2 tbsp. olive oil
- Crushed black pepper

- Add salt according to your need

Ingredients for the tortilla strips:

- 6 corn tortillas, 6- inches in size
- 1 ½ tbsp. canola oil
- ½ tsp. sea salt

Ingredients for the salad:

- 1 medium romaine lettuce head, roughly cut into 12-inch chunks
- 1/4-inch chopped bell pepper
- ½ red onion
- ½ jicama peeled
- 1 zucchini
- 4 tomatoes, seeded
- 4 ears corn
- 1 ½ cups canned black beans
- ½ cup chopped cilantro

Directions

1. Dressing: In a bowl, mix lime juice, garlic, honey, salt, and cumin until well combined.
2. Add oils one tbsp. at a time, constantly whisking with a spoon or tiny whisk as you go.
3. Season it with extra salt and pepper to taste if necessary. Separate yourself from the situation.
4. Set oven to 400°F for strips of corn tortilla.
5. On a cutting board, arrange the corn tortillas in a pyramid shape. Make a slit along the middle. Cut the stacks of halves into thin, 1 by 4-inch-thick strips, one on top of the other, widthwise.
6. Arrange the tortilla strips on a baking pan to keep them sticking together. Oil should be drizzled over the dish. Stir the veggies in the oil and season with salt and pepper to taste.
7. Allow to bake for 15 to 20 mins, stirring once every 5 mins, or till golden brown and crisp on the outside. Turn the heat on and let it cool for a few mins.
8. To prepare the salad, microwave the corn for three and a half mins, 2 ears at a time.
9. Take it off from oven and let sit for 5 mins with a hot pad.
10. Cut the bottom end of the corn off when it has cooled, approximately one and a half inches from the end. Remove the husk and silks by pulling them apart. Remove the husks from the kernels and place them in a bowl.
11. In a large bowl, combine the corn and remaining salad ingredients. To mix, give everything a good stir. Make sure all the ingredients are well-coated by adding the dressing and stirring well. If using, garnish with leaves of cilantro.
12. If you're serving with the tortilla strips, sprinkle some on top or offer them to your guests in a bowl to go with their meal.

Nutritional facts:
Calories: 228 Kcal proteins: 5 g fats: 8 g carbs: 35 g

6.10 Mediterranean grilled salmon kabobs

Prepping time: 15 mins, Cooking time: 06 mins, marinade time: 20 mins, servings: 4

Ingredients

- 2 lb. salmon fillet
- ⅓ cup olive oil
- 4 cloves garlic
- ½ tsp. cumin
- ½ tsp. chili powder
- ¼ tsp. coriander
- 1 tsp. thyme
- 1 tsp. oregano
- ¼ tsp. red chilies flakes
- 1 tsp. dill
- 1 tsp. sea salt
- ½ tsp. powdered black pepper
- 1 zucchini
- 3 fresh lemons
- 1/3 cup of grape tomatoes
- 1 fresh red onion

Directions

1. Peel and cut the salmon fillet into 1-to-2-inch pieces. Remove the seeds from 2 lemons before juicing and slicing. Cut thin slices of zucchini and red onion with a mandolin.
2. All the ingredients, including the drained dry spices, lemon juice, and olive oil, should be combined in a large prep basin and mixed well. Cover with the foil and marinate for around 20 mins to 2 hours in a fridge.
3. Coat 6-to-12-inch metal skewers with cooking spray after the salmon and vegetables have marinated. Thread the fish and vegetables alternately onto the skewers. The kabobs will still taste great without it, but it will make them look nicer.
4. Heat your grill to 350°F and coat with cooking spray. Put the kabobs onto the grill and cook for 3 to 5 mins on each side once it has heated up. When the salmon is cooked, it will be pink and have some char marks on it. Take off the kabobs from the grill and top with tzatziki sauce while they're still hot. Enjoy!

Nutritional facts:
Calories: 316 Kcal proteins: 30.4 g fats: 20.7 g carbs: 4.3 g

6.11 Low carb zucchini lasagna

Prepping time: 30 mins, cooking time: 01 hour, servings: 4

Ingredients

- 16 oz. ground beef
- 2 zucchinis
- 4 onions
- 2 cloves garlic
- 1 serrano pepper
- 3 tomatoes
- 5 oz. mushrooms
- ½ cube chicken bouillon
- ½ cup shredded mozzarella
- 1 tsp. paprika
- 1 tsp. dried thyme
- 1 tsp. dried basil
- A small amount of salt and pepper
- Cooking spray

Directions

1. Cut 1/2-inch-thick slices of zucchini by using a julienne peeler. Allow sitting for 10 mins after sprinkling with salt.
2. Using a paper towel, pat the zucchini slices dry. Cook for 3 mins at a high temperature on the grill or under the broiler in the oven.
3. Place the grilled or roasted zucchini on a plate lined with paper towels.
4. Tomatoes should have their stems removed and a cross inserted into the tops. After a few mins in boiling water, plunge them into ice water to stop the cooking process. Canned tomatoes are an option as well.
5. Remove stems and seeds from onions and garlic; finely chop all the above ingredients.
6. Garlic, onion, and chili should be fried in a large pan sprayed with cooking spray for one min.
7. Tomatoes, mushrooms, and garlic should be added to the pan at this point and cooked for another 4 mins. Afterward, remove them from the stove and put them aside.
8. The meat and paprika should be cooked together until completely browned in the same pan as the vegetables.
9. If desired, return the veggies to the pan and season with the rest of the chicken bouillon cubes and spices. For 25 mins at low heat, let the sauce simmer.
10. Set oven to 375°F.
11. Use one-third of zucchini to create a layer on the base of a small baking pan lined with parchment paper. On top of it, spoon about one-third of the beef sauce over the top. Continue layering the zucchini until you've used up all of the sauce and zucchini.
12. Bake for around 35 mins and then top with shredded mozzarella.
13. Allow the lasagna to cool for 10 mins after it has been taken out from the oven.

Nutritional facts:
Calories: 244 Kcal proteins: 30.4 g fats: 7.9 g carbs: 12.3 g

6.12 Easy quinoa salad

Prepping time: 10 mins, Cooking time: 10 mins, servings: 6

Ingredients

For the dressing:

- 1/4 cup olive oil
- 1 clove garlic
- 2 tbsp. lemon juice
- 1 tbsp. champagne vinegar
- 1 tsp. honey
- Kosher salt and black pepper for taste

For the salad:

- 2 cups cooked quinoa
- 2 cups chopped fresh spinach
- 1 cup crushed cucumber
- ½ cup grapes
- 1 large avocado
- 2 onions, sliced
- Kosher salt and black pepper for taste

Directions

1. Prepare the dressing first. Whisk the olive oil, lemon juice, honey, garlic, vinegar, salt, and pepper together in a dish. Place on the back burner.
2. Toss quinoa, avocado, spinach, cucumber, green onions, and tomatoes in a large bowl to mix.
3. Toss salad till well-coated with dressing. If desired, season salt and pepper to taste.

Nutritional facts:
Calories: 225 Kcal proteins: 4 g fats: 15 g carbs: 19 g

6.13 Cauliflower tacos

Prepping time: 10 mins, Cooking time: 40 mins, servings: 4

Ingredients

- 1 head cauliflower
- 1 tbsp. olive oil
- 2 tsp. taco seasoning

Avocado lime sauce

- 1 avocado
- 1 lime, juice and zest
- ½ tsp. kosher salt

For serving

- Tortillas
- feta cheese
- Red onions

Directions

Roast cauliflower

1. Set the oven to 425°F.
2. Make florets of cauliflower by cutting them into small, even pieces.
3. Season the cauliflower with taco spice after drizzling it with olive oil. Distribute on a wide baking sheet and toss to coat with spices evenly. If necessary, roast the cauliflower in two pans to prevent it from burning or being overcrowded.
4. Roast for 30 to 40 mins, turning once while cooking, till tender and golden.

Make the avocado lime sauce

1. Blend ripe avocado in a blender till smooth. Then combine lime juice, salt, and zest, scraping down the sides as necessary. Add 1 tbsp. of cold water to the thin down sauce, if necessary.

Assemble

1. You may use tortillas to serve the cauliflower tacos. Top with the pickled red onions, cilantro, and cheese, then drizzle with the avocado sauce.

Nutritional facts
Calories: 147 Kcal proteins: 3 g fats: 11 g carbs: 11 g

6.14 Slow cooker chicken noodle soup (a healthy meal option!)

Prepping time: 10 mins, cooking time: 03 hours, servings: 6

Ingredients

- 1 ½ lb. boneless chicken breasts
- 1 tsp. sea salt
- 1/4 tsp. powdered black pepper
- 4 cloves garlic
- 1 yellow onion
- 4 carrots, sliced
- 3 stalks celery, sliced
- 8 cups chicken broth
- 1 bay leaf
- 2 zucchinis
- 1 tsp. thyme
- 1 tsp. rosemary
- 1 tbsp. lemon juice
- 2 tbsp. chopped Italian parsley

Directions

1. Mix freshly ground black pepper and kosher salt to season the chicken.
2. Slow-cook seasoned chicken in a covered slow cooker for a couple of hours on low.
3. Toss in the other ingredients, including the carrots, celery, onion and garlic.
4. Cook for 6 to 8 hours on low or 4 to 5 hours on high, add the bay leaf and simmer till the chicken is done and the veggies are soft.
5. Retrieve cooked chicken from a slow cooker and shred it with two forks.
6. Spiralize the zucchini and combine with the thyme and rosemary in a large bowl until well-combined.
7. Cover the slow cooker and simmer it on low heat for a further 8 to 10 mins, or until the zucchini is done.
8. Stir in lemon juice and parsley.

Nutritional facts:
Calories: 226 Kcal proteins: 32 g fats: 5 g carbs: 14 g

6.15 No-cook zucchini noodles with pesto

Prepping time: 15 mins, cooking time: 01 min, servings: 5

Ingredients

- 4 zucchinis
- ½ tsp. salt
- 1 tbsp. olive oil
- ½ cup pesto
- 1 cup crushed cherry tomatoes
- For taste, ground pepper
- For taste, ground parmesan
- Coarse salt

Directions

1. To make long strands of zucchini use a spiralizer.
2. Drain noodles in a colander over a big bowl. Toss in the remaining 12 tsp. salt after adding the vegetables to the bowl. Allow for 10 mins of resting time.
3. Thoroughly rinse and squeeze away any remaining moisture.
4. Mix the zucchini with the olive oil in the basin until well-coated.
5. Toss in the pesto to ensure that everything is well-coated.
6. Serve in four spaghetti dishes, with zucchini divided among them. Add a sprinkling of diced tomato on top, if desired. Sprinkle with parmesan, pepper, and sea salt, if necessary.

Nutritional facts:
Calories: 242 Kcal proteins: 7 g fats: 19 g carbs: 10 g

6.16 Turkey-stuffed bell peppers

Prepping time: 30 mins, cooking time: 20 min, servings: 5

Ingredients

- 5 green chilies
- 2 tsp. olive oil
- 1 1/4 lb. ground turkey
- 1 chopped onion
- 1 clove of garlic
- 2 tsp. ground cumin
- 1 tsp. Italian seasoning
- 1/2 tsp. salt
- 1/2 tsp. pepper
- 2 chopped tomatoes
- 1 3/4 cups cheese
- 1 1/2 cups breadcrumbs
- 1/4 tsp. paprika

Directions

1. Set the oven at 325°F. Remove seeds by halving the peppers lengthwise. Put in a cooking spray-coated 15 by 10 by 1-inch pan.
2. Put the oil in a skillet over a flame. Using a medium skillet, cook and crumble turkey till no longer pink, about 6 to 8 mins. Allow cooling. Add the tomato sauce, cheese, and breadcrumbs, and mix everything well.
3. Make a filling using the turkey mixture and spoon it into the cavity. Add a pinch of paprika to the mixture. Bake uncovered for 20 to 25 minutes or until the filling is well cooked and the peppers soft.

Nutritional facts:
Calories: 323 Kcal proteins: 40 g fats: 10 g carbs: 20 g

6.17 Tropical chicken cauliflower rice bowls

Prepping time: 50 mins, cooking time: 10 min, servings: 4

Ingredients

- 1 pineapple, cubed, cored and peeled
- 1/2 cup Greek yogurt
- 1/2 cup and 2 tbsp. chopped cilantro
- 3 tbsp. lime juice
- 3/4 tsp. salt
- 1/4 tsp. chopped red pepper
- 1/8 tsp. chili powder
- 4 boneless chicken breasts
- 3 cups cauliflower florets
- 1 tbsp. canola oil
- 1 chopped red onion

Directions

1. Use a blender to mix the marinade ingredients: 1 cup pineapple, 2 tbsp. cilantro and lime juice, 1/4 tsp. salt, pepper flakes, and chili powder. Combine chicken with the marinade in a large basin; cover and chill for 1 to 3 hours in the refrigerator.
2. Process the cauliflower till it resembles rice in a clean blender. Heat oil in a big pan at medium-high temperature. Cook onion for 3 to 5 mins, or till it's gently brown. Simmer and toss the cauliflower for 5 to 7 mins, till it is just beginning to brown. Put the broccoli and cook for an additional 2-3 mins. Cook, covered, on medium heat for 3-5 mins till cauliflower is soft. Mix in 1 cup of pineapple and the rest lime juice and salt. Add the rest of the cilantro and mix well. Take care of yourself by staying warm.
3. Prepare the grill or the broiler by preheating it. Remove chicken from marinade and discard the marinade. Grill the chicken on medium heat on an oil grill rack. Broil 4 inches from fire for 4 to 6 mins each side or till a thermometer reads 165°F. Slice after 5 mins of resting.
4. Place cauliflower mixture in four bowls and serve. Add the leftover chicken, coconut, pineapple, and lime wedges, if necessary.

Nutritional facts:
Calories: 325 Kcal proteins: 38 g fats: 10 g carbs: 22 g

6.18 Slow-cooker pork chops

Prepping time: 15 mins, cooking time: 02 hours, servings: 4

Ingredients

- 1/2 cup flour
- 1/2 tsp. ground mustard
- 1/2 tsp. garlic pepper blend
- 1/4 tsp. seasoned salt
- 4 boneless chopped pork loins
- 2 tbsp. canola oil
- 1 can chicken broth

Directions

1. Combine 1/4 cup of flour, mustard, seasoned salt, and garlic pepper in a small basin. Place the pork chops and dredge one by one to coat. Chops should be browned on all sides in oil in a big pan.
2. Move to a 5-quart slow cooker and simmer on low for several hours. On the chops, pour the broth. At low heat cook the meat for couple of hours, covered, until its fork tender.
3. Cook pork until it reaches an internal temperature of 145°F. Cook, covered with a lid, on high until the gravy has thickened, whisking in the remaining flour till smooth.

Nutritional facts:
Calories: 279 Kcal proteins: 24 g fats: 14 g carbs: 12 g

6.19 Sweet & tangy salmon with green beans

Prepping time: 20 mins, Cooking time: 15 mins, servings: 4

Ingredients

- 4 pieces salmon fillets
- 1 tbsp. butter
- 2 tbsp. brown sugar
- 2 tbsp. soy sauce
- 2 tbsp. Dijon mustard
- 1 tbsp. olive oil
- 1/2 tsp. pepper
- 1/8 tsp. salt
- 1 lb. green beans

Directions

1. To get started, set the oven to 425°F. Use cooking spray to coat a 15 by 10 by 1-inch baking pan and place the fillets in it. Mix all ingredients except for the oil and pepper in a small pan over low heat until well combined. On the salmon, apply half of the sauce mixture.
2. Mix green beans with the rest of the brown sugar mixture in a large mixing bowl until well-coated. Place the green beans all over the fish fillets on a serving dish. Roast for 14 to 16 mins, or till fish flakes readily when tested with the fork.

Nutritional facts
Calories: 394 Kcal proteins: 31 g fats: 22 g carbs: 17 g

6.20 Spaghetti squash meatball casserole

Prepping time: 35 mins, Cooking time: 30 mins, servings: 6

Ingredients

- 4 lb. spaghetti squash
- 1/2 tsp. salt
- 1/2 tsp. fennel seed
- 1/4 tsp. ground coriander
- 1/4 tsp. dried basil
- 1/4 tsp. dried oregano
- 1 lb. lean crushed beef
- 2 tsp. olive oil
- 1 chopped onion
- 1 clove of garlic
- 2 cups collard greens, chopped
- 1 cup chopped spinach
- 1 cup ricotta cheese
- 2 plum tomatoes, chopped
- 1 cup pasta sauce
- 1 cup mozzarella cheese

Directions

1. Split the squash in two lengthwise and remove the seeds before consuming. Split sides down and place half on the microwave-safe dish. For tenderness, cook on high for 15 to 20 mins in the microwave. Allow cooling.
2. Turn the oven on to 350°F. Combine the remaining spices and 1/4 tsp. salt; add to the beef and combine well. Make 1 1/2-inch ball out of the dough. Cook meatballs in a large frying pan until browned, then remove from pan and set aside to cool.
3. In the same pan, heat the oil medium heat and cook the onion for 3 to 4 mins, till it is soft. Cook and stir for one min after having added the garlic. Toss together spinach, collards greens, ricotta, & the remaining salt and then remove from heat.
4. Prepare spaghetti squash by scraping it with a fork; add to the green mixture. Bake in a 13 by 9-inch or 3-quart oiled baking dish. Add meatballs, sauce, and cheese to a plate. Bake for 30 to 35 mins, or till meatballs are well cooked.

Nutritional facts:
Calories: 362 Kcal proteins: 26 g fats: 16 g carbs: 32 g

6.21 Parmesan chicken with artichoke hearts

Prepping time: 20 mins, Cooking time: 20 mins, servings: 4

Ingredients

- 4 boneless chicken breasts
- 3 tsp. olive oil
- 1 tsp. crushed rosemary
- 1/2 tsp. dried thyme
- 1/2 tsp. pepper
- 2 cans of artichoke hearts
- 1 chopped onion
- 1/2 cup white wine
- 2 cloves garlic, chopped
- 1/4 cup parmesan cheese
- 8 slices of lemon
- 2 green onions, sliced

Directions

1. Set the oven to 375°F. Pour 1 1/2 tbsp. olive oil on chicken before placing in a 15 by 10 by a 1-inch baking pan. Sprinkle half of the rosemary, thyme, and pepper mixture over the chicken and toss to combine.
2. Toss together wine, artichoke hearts, garlic, onion, and the rest of the herb combination in a mixing bowl until well-coated. Set up a perimeter of pillows and blankets around the chicken. Lemon slices go on top of the chicken after it's been smothered with cheese.
3. Roast for 20-25 mins, till a meat thermometer registers at 165°F. Add a few slivers of green onion on top if desired.

Nutritional facts:
Calories: 339 Kcal proteins: 42 g fats: 9 g carbs: 18 g

6.22 Salmon & spinach salad with avocado

Prepping time: 25 mins, Cooking time: 01 mins, servings: 2

Ingredients

- 2 salmon fillets
- 1/4 tsp. salt
- 1/8 tsp. pepper
- 1 tsp. canola oil
- 4 cups baby spinach
- 2 tbsp. balsamic vinaigrette
- 1/2 ripe avocado
- 2 tbsp. dried cranberries
- 2 tbsp. sunflower kernels
- 2 tbsp. chopped walnuts

Directions

1. Add salt and pepper to the fish. Put the oil in a big frying pan on medium heat. Place the fillets skin-side-up and cook for 4 to 5 mins on each side or till the fish just starts to flake freely when tested with a fork.
2. Mix spinach with the vinaigrette in a big bowl and serve on two plates. Add the remaining ingredients and place fish on top of spinach.

Nutritional facts
Calories: 386 Kcal proteins: 23 g fats: 27 g carbs: 15 g

6.23 Shrimp avocado salad

Prepping time: 25 mins, Cooking Time: 20 mins, servings: 6

Ingredients

- 1 lb. chopped cooked shrimp
- 2 plum tomatoes, chopped
- 2 chopped onions
- 1/4 cup chopped onion
- 1 minced jalapeno pepper
- 1 minced serrano pepper
- 2 tbsp. minced cilantro
- 2 tbsp. lime juice
- 2 tbsp. rice vinegar seasoned
- 2 tbsp. olive oil
- 1 tsp. adobo seasoning
- 3 cubed ripe avocados
- Leaves of bibb lettuce
- Lime wedges

Directions

1. In a large mixing bowl, combine the first seven ingredients. Then add the adobo seasoning, oil, vinegar and lime juice combination to the shrimp mixture. Refrigerate for at least one hour and cover to enable flavors to combine.
2. Avocados may be added to your serving dish by gently stirring them in. Serve on top of leaves of lettuce or in lettuce, depending on your preference. Serve with the lime wedges for squeezing over the top.

Nutritional facts
Calories: 252 Kcal proteins: 17 g fats: 19 g carbs: 11 g

6.24 Pan-roasted chicken and vegetables

Prepping time: 15 mins, Cooking time: 45 mins, servings: 6

Ingredients

- 2 lb. large red potatoes, sliced
- 1 chopped onion
- 2 tbsp. olive oil
- 3 minced garlic cloves
- 1 1/4 tsp. salt
- 1 tsp. crushed rosemary
- 3/4 tsp. pepper
- 1/2 tsp. paprika
- 6 bone-in chicken thighs
- 6 cups baby spinach

Directions

1. Set the oven to 425°F. Fork-toss the potatoes with the onion in a huge bowl with the oil and garlic, season with the salt and pepper to taste, and sprinkle with the rosemary. Cooking spray on a baking pan will help prevent sticking.
2. Combine the paprika, rosemary, and the rest of the salt and pepper in a mixing bowl. Place chicken on a serving platter and top with the paprika mixture. Roast for 35-40 mins, or until the chicken reaches an internal temperature of 170-175°F, and the veggies are just soft.
3. Keep the chicken that has been transferred to a serving dish warm. Add spinach to the veggies before serving. For a further 8-10 mins, roast the veggies and spinach until they're fork-tender. Serve the veggies with the chicken after mixing them.

Nutritional facts:
Calories: 357 Kcal proteins: 28 g fats: 14 g carbs: 28 g

6.25 Spicy beef & pepper stir-fry

Prepping time: 20 mins, Cooking time: 10 mins, servings: 4

Ingredients

- 1 lb. beef sirloin steak
- 1 tbsp. minced gingerroot
- 3 cloves of garlic, minced
- 1/4 tsp. pepper
- 3/4 tsp. salt
- 1 cup coconut milk
- 2 tbsp. sugar
- 1 tbsp. hot sriracha sauce
- 1/2 tsp. lime zest
- 2 tbsp. lime juice
- 2 tbsp. canola oil
- 1 red pepper
- 1/2 red onion, thinly sliced
- 1 jalapeno pepper, thinly sliced
- 4 cups baby spinach
- 2 green onions, thinly sliced
- 2 tbsp. chopped cilantro

Directions

1. Mix ginger, two cloves of garlic, pepper, and 1/2 tsp. of salt with the meat in a large mixing bowl; leave for 15 mins. Add remaining salt and lime zest into a bowl and whisk together until well combined.
2. Heat 1 tbsp. of oil in a large pan at medium-high temperature. Stir-fry the meat for a further 2 to 3 mins, or till no longer pink in the middle. Take it out of the oven.
3. Reduce heat to medium-low and cook remaining veggies for a further 2 to 3 mins, often stirring, till crisp-tender (around 2-3 mins). Cook well after adding coconut milk. Then add the spinach and meat and simmer, turning periodically, till the spinach is mashed and the beef is cooked through. Add cilantro and green onions, if necessary.

Nutritional facts:
Calories: 312 Kcal proteins: 26g fats: 16g carbs: 15g

6.26 Pulled chicken sandwiches

Prepping time: 20 mins, cooking time: 04 hours, servings: 6

Ingredients

- 1 chopped onion
- 1 can tomato paste
- 1/4 cup chicken broth
- 2 tbsp. brown sugar
- 1 tbsp. cider vinegar
- 1 tbsp. yellow mustard
- 1 tbsp. Worcestershire sauce
- 2 cloves of garlic, minced
- 2 tsp. chili powder
- 3/4 tsp. salt
- 1/8 tsp. cayenne pepper
- 1 1/2 lb. boneless chicken breasts
- 6 wheat hamburgers, split

Directions

1. Combine the first eleven ingredients in a small dish. Slow-cook the chicken in a 3-quart pot according to the package directions. Top with sauce.
2. Cook the chicken for 4 to 5 hours on low heat. Once you've removed the chicken, let it cool for a few mins. 2 forks are ideal for shredding meat. Put everything back in the slow cooker and reheat until hot. To serve, place on each bun.

Nutritional facts:
Calories: 296 Kcal proteins: 29 g fats: 5 g carbs: 35 g

6.27 Skillet pork chops with apples and onion

Prepping time: 20 mins, Cooking Time: 20 mins, servings: 6

Ingredients

- 4 pork loin chops, boneless
- 3 apples
- Thin wedges of 1 onion
- 1/4 cup water
- 1/3 cup balsamic vinaigrette
- 1/2 tsp. salt
- 1/4 tsp. pepper

Directions

1. Brown the pork chops on all sides in a big nonstick pan on medium heat for approximately 4 mins. Take it out of the pan.
2. Add apples, onion, and water to the same pan and add pork chops to the apple mix. Drizzle vinaigrette on the pork chops. Add a pinch of salt and a few grinds of black pepper to taste. Simmer, covered, for 3 to 5 mins or till the temperature of chop reaches 145°F.

Nutritional Facts:
Calories: 360 Kcal proteins: 33 g fats: 15 g carbs: 22 g

6.28 Ginger steak fried rice

Prepping time: 30 mins, Cooking Time: 20 mins, servings: 4

Ingredients

- 2 large eggs, lightly beaten
- 2 tsp. olive oil
- 1 beef sirloin steak (3/4 pound), cut into thin strips
- 4 tbsp. reduced-sodium soy sauce, divided
- 1 package (12 ounces) broccoli coleslaw mix
- 1 cup frozen peas
- 2 tbsp. grated fresh ginger root
- 3 garlic cloves, minced
- 2 cups cooked brown rice
- 4 green onions, sliced

Directions

1. Cook and whisk eggs till no liquid is left in a big nonstick pan sprayed with cooking spray, breaking them up into tiny pieces. Wipe the pan if required after removing it.
2. Heat the oil in the same pan at a medium-high temperature until shimmering. Stir-fry the beef for 1-2 mins or till it is no longer pink in the center. Remove from heat & add 1 tbsp. of soy sauce.
3. Cook and toss the coleslaw mixture till it is crisp-tender, then add the peas, ginger, and garlic to the same pan. Continue to heat the mixture after adding rice and the rest of the soy sauce and stirring to incorporate. Cooked eggs, meat, and green onions may all be added at this point.

Nutritional facts:
Calories: 346 Kcal proteins: 29g fats: 9g carbs: 36g

6.29 Italian hot dish

Prepping time: 30 mins, Cooking time: 40 mins, servings: 4

Ingredients

- 1 1/2 cups uncooked pasta
- 1 lb. ground beef
- 1 cup sliced mushrooms
- 1/2 cup chopped onion
- 1/2 cup chopped green chilis
- 1 tsp. dried oregano
- 1/2 tsp. garlic powder
- 1/4 tsp. onion powder
- 1/8 tsp. pepper
- 1 can tomato sauce
- 1/2 cup mozzarella cheese
- 2 tbsp. parmesan cheese

Directions

1. Turn the oven on to 350°F. To prepare al dente pasta, follow the package instructions and drain.
2. Cook and shred the beef with 1/2 cup of mushrooms, an onion, and green pepper in a big pan sprayed using cooking spray till no longer pink, 5-7 mins. Bring to the boil, and then remove from heat. Simmer for 15 mins, covered, on low heat.
3. Cook the pasta according to the package directions in an 8-inch baking dish sprayed using cooking spray. Add the leftover meat sauce and mushrooms to the dish. Add 1 tbsp. of parmesan cheese and 1/4 cup of mozzarella cheese on top.
4. Bake for 35 mins in the oven with the lid on. Remove the lid and top with the rest of the cheese. Bake for 5-10 mins, till cheese is melted, or till thoroughly cooked through.

Nutritional facts:
Calories: 394 Kcal proteins: 34g fats: 15g carbs: 32g

6.30 Grilled beef chimichangas

Prepping time: 25 Mins, Cooking Time: 10 Mins, Servings: 6

Ingredients

- 1 lb. ground beef
- 1 chopped onion
- 2 cloves of garlic
- 1 can chop green chilies
- 1/4 cup salsa
- 1/4 tsp. ground cumin
- 6 tortillas
- 3/4 cup cheese
- Sour cream and guacamole, optional

Directions

1. In a large pan, cook meat, onion, and garlic till no further pink and onion are soft, breaking up the meat into pieces as it cooks; drain. Add the chilies, salsa, and cumin to the bowl. Stir well to combine.
2. Top each tortilla with 2 tbsp. of cheese and 1/2 cup of the meat mixture. Roll up the tortilla, folding in the bottom and the edges over the filling as you go.
3. Grill the chimichangas with the seam facing up. Allow to cook for 10-12 mins till crisp and browned, flipping once while cooking. Serve with guacamole and sour cream, if necessary.

Nutritional facts:
Calories: 295 Kcal proteins: 22g fats: 12g carbs: 25g

6.31 In-a-pinch chicken and spinach

Prepping time: 25 mins, Cooking Time: 20 mins, servings: 4

Ingredients

- 4 boneless chicken breasts
- 2 tbsp. olive oil
- 1 tbsp. butter
- 6 ounces baby spinach
- 1 cup salsa

Directions

1. Use a meat mallet to pound the chicken to a thickness of 1/2 inch. Over medium heat, combine the oil and butter in a big pan, and cook the chicken. Fry the chicken till it is no pinker on both sides, about 5-6 mins on each side. Warm-up by removing and storing in a warm place.
2. Cook and stir for 3-4 mins, or till the spinach has wilted, with spinach and salsa in a pan. Serve with fried chicken, if necessary.

Nutritional facts
Calories: 297 Kcal proteins: 36g fats: 14g carbs: 6g

6.32 The Great Lasagna

Prepping time: 30 mins, Cooking time: 40 mins, servings: 8

Ingredients

- 9 lasagna sheets
- 1 lb. ground beef
- 1 chopped zucchini
- 1 chopped onion
- 1 chopped green pepper
- 3 cloves of garlic
- 1 jar of sauce of meatless pasta
- 1 can diced tomatoes
- 1/2 cup chopped basil leaves
- 2 tbsp. ground flaxseed
- 5 tsp. Italian seasoning
- 1/4 tsp. pepper

- 1 carton ricotta cheese
- 1 package of chopped frozen spinach, thawed and squeezed dry
- 1 egg, casually beaten
- 2 tbsp. balsamic vinegar
- 2 cups mozzarella cheese
- 1/4 cup parmesan cheese

Directions

3. Preheat oven to 350°F. Cook noodles according to package directions. Meanwhile, in a 6-quart stockpot, cook beef, zucchini, onion, and green pepper over medium heat until beef is no longer pink, breaking beef into pieces. Add garlic, cook 1 min longer and drain.
4. Stir in pasta sauce, diced tomatoes, basil, flax, Italian seasoning and pepper, heat through. Drain noodles and rinse in cold water.
5. In a small bowl, mix ricotta cheese, spinach, egg, and vinegar. Spread 1 cup meat mixture into a 13-by-9-inch. Spray cooking spray on the baking dish. Add three lasagna sheets, two cups of the meat mixture, one and a quarter cup of the ricotta cheese mix, and two-thirds of a cup of mozzarella cheese to the top of the sheets. Layers should be repeated. Top with remaining sheets, meat mixture and mozzarella cheese; sprinkle with parmesan cheese.
6. Bake, covered, for 30 mins. Bake, uncovered, for 10-15 mins longer or until cheese is melted. Let sit for 10 mins before serving.

Nutritional facts
Calories: 392 Kcal proteins: 32 g fats: 12 g carbs: 39 g

6.33 Simple sesame chicken with couscous

Prepping time: 25 mins, Cooking Time: 20 mins, servings: 4

Ingredients

- 1 1/2 cups water
- 1 cup wheat couscous, uncooked
- 1 tbsp. olive oil
- 2 cups coleslaw mix
- 4 onions, sliced
- 1/2 cup and 2 tbsp. of toasted sesame salad dressing
- 2 cups cooked chicken breast
- 2 tbsp. minced cilantro
- Chopped peanuts

Directions

1. Water should be brought to a boil in a small pot. Add the couscous and mix well. Keep covered for 5-10 mins or till water is evaporated after removing from heat. Use a fork to fluff.
2. Heat the oil in a big, nonstick frying pan on medium heat. Cook and whisk the coleslaw mix for 3-4 mins, or till it is barely soft. Toss in the green onions, with 2 tbsp. of the dressing and couscous, and cook until the greens are tender. Keep heated couscous that has been removed from the pan.
3. Cook and stir chicken and remaining dressing in the same frying pan until cooked through. Remove from heat. Top with the cilantro and peanuts if preferred and serve over couscous.

Nutritional facts

Calories: 320 Kcal proteins: 26 g fats: 9 g carbs: 35 g

6.34 Braised Pork Stew

Prepping time: 30 mins, Cooking Time: 20 mins, servings: 4

Ingredients

- 1 lb. pork tenderloin
- 1/2 tsp. salt
- 1/2 tsp. pepper
- 5 tbsp. flour
- 1 tbsp. olive oil
- 16 oz. different frozen vegetables
- 1 1/2 cups chicken broth
- 2 cloves garlic
- 2 tsp. mustard
- 1 tsp. dried thyme
- 2 tbsp. water

Directions

7. Sprinkle pork with salt and pepper; add 3 tbsp. flour and toss to coat. In a large skillet, heat oil over medium heat. Brown pork. Drain if necessary. Stir in vegetables, broth, garlic, mustard, and thyme. Bring to a boil. Reduce heat; simmer, covered, until pork and vegetables are tender, 10-15 mins.
8. In a small bowl, mix remaining flour and water until smooth; stir into stew. Return to a boil, stirring constantly; cook and stir until thickened, 1-2 mins.

Nutritional facts

Calories: 250 Kcal Proteins: 26 g fats: 8 g carbs: 16 g

6.35 Asparagus Nicoise Salad

Prepping time: 20 mins, Cooking Time: 20 mins, servings: 4

Ingredients

- 1 lb. potatoes
- 1 lb. asparagus
- 3 pouches of albacore fish
- 1/2 cup olives, optional
- 1/2 cup zesty Italian salad dressing

Directions

1. Put the potatoes in a big pot and cover them with 2 inches of water. Put over high heat and bring the mixture to a rapid boil. Reduce the heat to medium-low and boil the potatoes for 10-12 mins, stirring

occasionally. Add the asparagus for the final 2-4 mins of the cooking. Drain the potatoes and asparagus, and then plunge them into a large bowl of cold water.
2. When ready to serve, remove potatoes and asparagus from the water and wipe dry before evenly dividing among 4 dinner plates. Add tuna and olives to taste. Dress the dish by drizzling it with dressing.

Nutritional facts
Calories: 233 Kcal proteins: 16 g fats: 8 g carbs: 23 g

6.36 Peppered tuna kabobs

Prepping time: 30 mins, Cooking Time: 20 mins, servings: 4

Ingredients

- 1/2 cup frozen corn
- 4 chopped onions
- 1 chopped jalapeno pepper
- 2 tbsp. chopped parsley
- 2 tbsp. lime juice
- 1 lb. tuna steaks
- 1 tsp. ground pepper
- 2 red peppers, cut into pieces
- 1 mango, 1-inch cubes

Directions

1. Set aside the first 5 ingredients for the salsa inside a small dish.
2. Pepper the tuna well before cooking. Rotate threading onto 4 metal or wet wooden skewers while cooking.
3. Grease the grill rack and place the skewers on it. Cook the tuna and peppers for 10-12 mins, covered, in a medium saucepan, stirring periodically, till the tuna is medium-rare and the peppers are soft. Combine the dish with a side of salsa to complete the meal.

Nutritional facts
Calories: 205 Kcal proteins: 29 g fats: 2 g carbs: 20 g

6.37 Makeover Turkey Burgers with Peach Mayo

Prepping time: 25 mins, Cooking Time: 20 mins, servings: 6

Ingredients

- 1 1/2 tsp. canola oil
- 2 chopped peaches
- 1/2 tsp. minced gingerroot
- 4 tsp. teriyaki sauce
- 1/4 cup red onion, chopped
- 1/2 tsp. pepper
- 1/4 tsp. salt
- 1 1/2 lb. ground turkey
- 1/3 cup mayonnaise
- 6 toasted hamburger buns

Directions

1. Heat the oil in a large pan at a medium-high temperature until shimmering and fragrant. Cook and stir the peaches and ginger till they are soft. Cook for one additional min after adding 1 tsp. teriyaki sauce. Cool gently in a small dish.
2. Mix onion, salt, pepper, and the rest of the teriyaki sauce in a mixing bowl. Add the turkey and gently fold it in, but make sure it's well combined. Make six 1/2-inch-thick patties out of the mixture.
3. To gently coat the grill rack, wet the paper towel using cooking oil and massage it with long-handled tongs. When grilling, use medium heat and cover, broil the hamburgers for 5-6 mins on all sides, or till a meat thermometer registers 165°F.
4. The peach mixture should be mixed with mayonnaise. Peach mayo and any preferred toppings should be served on buns with the burgers.

Nutritional facts:
Calories: 319 Kcal proteins: 25 g fats: 14 g carbs: 25 g

6.38 Sesame Turkey Stir-Fry

Prepping time: 25 mins, Cooking Time: 20 mins, servings: 4

Ingredients

- 1 tsp. cornstarch
- 1/2 cup water
- 2 tbsp. soy sauce
- 1 tbsp. honey
- 2 tsp. curry powder
- 1/8 tsp. crushed red chilies flakes
- 2 tsp. canola oil
- 1 red pepper
- 1 onion
- 1 clove of garlic
- 2 cups cooked turkey breast
- 1 green onion
- 2 cups brown rice, cooked

Directions

1. Mix the first 6 ingredients in a bowl until well-combined. Set aside. Heat the oil in a large skillet on medium heat. Stir in the red pepper and onion, and cook till they are crisp-tender, about 3 mins. Sauté the garlic for a further 30 seconds before adding it back in.
2. Add the cornstarch mixture to the pan once it has been stirred. To thicken, cook for 2 mins, stirring constantly. Bring to the boil. Cook the turkey until well heated, stirring occasionally. Add the green onion and mix well. Serve over rice if necessary. Add a few dashes of sriracha and sesame seeds, if necessary.

Nutritional facts:
Calories: 269 Kcal proteins: 25 g fats: 4 g carbs: 32 g

6.39 Beef and Rice Stuffed Cabbage Rolls

Prepping time: 20 mins, cooking time: 06 hours, servings: 6

Ingredients

- 12 cabbage leaves
- 1 cup brown rice, cooked
- 1/4 cup chopped onion
- 1 egg, casually beaten

Sauce:

- 1 can tomato sauce
- 1 tbsp. brown sugar
- 1/4 cup milk
- 1/2 tsp. salt
- 1/4 tsp. pepper
- 1 lb. lean beef

- 1 tbsp. lemon juice
- 1 tsp. Worcestershire sauce

Directions

1. Cook the cabbage in boiling water for 3-5 mins, depending on how crisp or tender you want it. Cook the cabbage in batches. Drain and let it cool for a few mins. Make a v-shaped incision through the thick vein at the base of each cabbage leaf.
2. Mix rice, milk, onion, salt, egg, and pepper in a large mixing bowl. Add the meat and carefully combine, but do not overmix. Each cabbage leaf should have approximately a quarter cup of the meat mixture on it. Fold over the filling and bring together the leaf's cut edges. Roll up, tucking in the ends.
3. Place 6 rolls in a 4 or 5 quart slow cooker. Combine all of the sauce ingredients in a dish and serve half of it over the cabbage rolls. Add the remaining rolls and sauce to the plate. For 6-8 hours, cook on low with the lid till the meat thermometer registers 160°F and the cabbage is cooked. Beef should be tender.

Nutritional facts
Calories: 204 Kcal proteins: 18 g fats: 7 g carbs: 16 g

6.40 Meaty Slow-Cooked Jambalaya

Prepping time: 05 mins, cooking time: 7 hours 15 mins, servings: 12

Ingredients

- 1 can diced tomatoes
- 1 cup chicken broth
- 1 chopped green pepper
- 1 chopped onion
- 2 celery ribs in sliced form
- 1/2 cup white wine
- 4 cloves of garlic
- 2 tsp. Cajun seasoning
- 2 tsp. parsley flakes
- 1 tsp. dried basil
- 1 tsp. dried oregano
- 3/4 tsp. salt
- 1/2 to 1 tsp. cayenne pepper
- 2 lb. boneless chicken thighs
- 1 package cooked andouille
- 2 lb. uncooked shrimp

- 8 cups brown rice, cooked

Directions

1. Mix the first thirteen ingredients in a big dish. Cook the chicken and sausage in a 6-quart slow cooker. On top of it, pour the tomato mixture. Cook on low for 7-9 hours, covered, till chicken is fork tender.
2. Add the shrimp and mix well. Allow cooking till the shrimp are pink and opaque in the middle, about another 15-20 mins. Serve over rice if desired.

Nutritional facts
Calories: 387 Kcal proteins: 36 g fats: 10 g carbs: 37 g

6.41 Slow Cooker Boeuf Bourguignon

Prepping time: 30 mins, cooking time: 08 hours, servings: 12

Ingredients

- 3 lb. beef meat
- 1 3/4 cups red wine
- 3 tbsp. olive oil
- 3 tbsp. dried onion
- 2 tbsp. parsley flakes
- 1 bay leaf
- 1 tsp. dried thyme
- 1/4 tsp. pepper
- 8 chopped bacon strips
- 1 lb. mushrooms
- 24 onions
- 2 cloves of garlic
- 1/3 cup flour
- 1 tsp. salt

Directions

1. In a big, airtight container, add the meat, wine, oil, and spices. Coat thoroughly and refrigerate overnight, covering it.
2. Cook bacon till crisp in a large pan on medium heat, turning periodically. Drain over paper towels after removing them with the slotted spoon. Remove drippings, keeping 1 tbsp. in the pan.
3. Add the mushrooms and onions to the drippings and simmer, often stirring, till they are soft and translucent for about 10 mins. Sauté the garlic for a further 30 seconds before adding it back in.
4. Remove meat from marinade and place it in a 4-to-5-quart slow cooker. Reserve marinade. Toss the meat with flour and salt to cover it completely in the sauce. Add the bacon and mushroom combination to the top to complete the look. Add the marinade that was reserved.
5. For 8 to 10 hours, or until the meat is cooked, place the pot in the oven with the lid on and cook low. Take out the bay leaf before you begin. Noodles may be added to the stew if desired.

Nutritional facts:
Calories: 289 Kcal proteins: 25 g fats: 15 g carbs: 8 g

Conclusion

Type 2 diabetes is characterized by difficulties in delivering sufficient glucose to the cells. Diabetes problems such as nerve, kidney, & eye damage plus cardiovascular disease may occur when the sugar doesn't get to where it's meant to be in the body.

Complex carbs such as vegetables, beans, brown rice, quinoa, oatmeal, whole wheat, fruits, & lentils are included in a type 2 diabetes diet meal plan. Simple carbs like sugar, white bread, pasta, and wheat, as well as cookies and pastries, should be avoided.

Blood sugar levels increase relatively little after eating glycemic index load (low index) foods; hence they are preferable alternatives for people with diabetes. Type 2 diabetes long-term consequences may be prevented with good glycemic control.

Even though fats don't directly affect blood sugar levels, they may help decrease their absorption.

Protein is a good source of long-lasting energy that has little impact on blood sugar levels. It helps maintain blood sugar levels consistently and reduces sugar cravings and the sense of being full when a meal is finished. You can get a lot of protein from legumes and grains, birds and meats like tofu, and dairy products such as cheese and yogurt.

Chia seeds, cinnamon, wild salmon, balsamic vinegar, and lentils are five diabetic "superfoods" to consume.

Vegetables are an important part of a healthy diabetic diet plan, and processed sweets and red meat should be minimized.

In addition to vegetarian or vegan diets, the Diabetes Association of America (which stresses activity) & the Paleo Diet are all recommended for patients with type 2 diabetes.

Type 2 diabetics should follow dietary recommendations that include low glycemic load carbs, mostly from vegetables, as well as lipids and proteins derived predominantly from plant sources, according to the American Diabetes Association.

Sugary drinks (regular & diet), processed carbohydrates, refined sugars, trans fatty acids and any processed foods should be avoided by people with type 2 diabetes. Other foods to avoid include high-fat dairy products & meats, high-fat dairy products, high fructose corn syrup, artificial sweeteners.